Norton
STORY

Bob Holliday

Patrick Stephens, Cambridge

First published – 1972

Reprinted – 1973

Second Edition – 1976

ISBN 0 85059 246 1

Text set in 10 on 11 pt Times Roman.
Printed on M6 Cartridge 94 gsm by
Blackfriars Press of Leicester and bound by
Hunter & Foulis Ltd of Edinburgh for
the publishers, Patrick Stephens Ltd, Bar Hill,
Cambridge, CB3 8EL.

Contents

Illustrations

Diagrams in Text

Norton Story in brief

1869 James Lansdowne Norton born.

1898 Norton Manufacturing Co Ltd formed.

1902 Norton 'motorised' bicycle launched.

1907 H. Rem Fowler won the twin-cylinder class of the first TT.

1908 Big Four Norton put on the market.

1911 490 cc 3½ hp model introduced.

1913 Company reconstituted as Norton Motors Ltd.

1914 D. R. O'Donovan began speed tests of Brooklands Specials.

1920 Factory moved to Bracebridge Street, Birmingham.

1922 First appearance of the 490 cc overhead valve machine.

1923 Bert Denly raised Hour record to 85.22 mph.

1924 The Year of Firsts, including Senior and Sidecar TT wins.

1925 Death, at 56, of James Norton; first Norton IoM 1-2-3 was scored in the Amateur TT.

1926 Joe Craig joined the experimental department.

1927 First ohc engine gained Alec Bennett Senior TT victory; Denly covered more than 100 miles in an hour.

1928 350 cc Junior machines introduced.

1930 Arthur Carroll re-designed the ohc engines.

1931 Jim Simpson first to lap TT course at over 80 mph; Bill Lacey raised Hour record to 110.80 mph.

1932 International Model introduced; Senior TT hat-trick for second year running.

1933 Hat-tricks in both Junior and Senior TTs.

1934 Hairpin valve springs for racing machines.

1935 Jimmy Guthrie raised Hour record to 114.09 mph.

1936 Plunger rear springing used for first time.

1937 Double overhead camshaft engines for racing machines; Freddie Frith lifted TT lap record over 90 mph.

1938 Harold Daniell set 91 mph TT lap record that stood for 12 years.

1939 Nortons 'temporarily withdrawn' from competitions to concentrate on military work.

1945 C. Gilbert Smith became managing director.

1947 Bill and Dennis Mansell left Nortons.

1948 Dominator twin and 500T trials mount at Earls Court Show.

1950 Loop-type Featherbed frames adopted for works racers; Geoff Duke headed double TT hat-trick.

1951 Manx 30M and 40M models had Featherbed frames.

1952 Norton Motors Ltd merged with Associated Motor Cycles Ltd.

1953 Ray Amm raised Hour record to more than 133 mph.

1954 Eric Oliver won first post-war Sidecar TT; production of special racing machines ended.

1955 Side valve machines discontinued after 45 years of production.

1956 International models built only to special order.

1957 After one year in retirement Joe Craig died in a car accident.

1958 Norton Diamond Jubilee celebrated by introduction of the 250 cc Jubilee twin.

1959 Desmodromic valves tried in the IoM.

1960 'Low boy' headless frame experiment tried in TT practising.

1961 Mike Hailwood won Senior TT at over 100 mph average—first and only time with a 'single'; quantity production of Manx models ceased.

1963 Bracebridge Street factory closed; work transferred to Matchless premises at Woolwich; 750 cc Atlas model introduced.

1965 Norton riders won both Manufacturers' and Club TT team prizes.

1966 Norton Villiers Ltd formed; all Norton and AMC racing equipment sold.

1967 Norton Commando 750 cc 'Isolastic' model exhibited at Earls Court Show.

1968 Commandos reached home market.

1969 Matchless premises at Woolwich closed; Commando engine production moved to Villiers factory, Wolverhampton; new NV building opened at Andover, Hants.

1970 Peter Williams and Charlie Sanby won Thruxton 500-mile endurance Grand Prix on a Commando.

1972 Formation of John Player-Norton racing team.

1973 Absorption of BSA-Triumph to form Norton Villiers Triumph; Peter Williams won Formula 750 TT at 105.47 mph.

1975 Cosworth-engined Norton Challenge made its debut; death of Bill Mansell, aged 86.

Preface

A legend in one word

'WHAT, ANOTHER BOOK about Norton motor-cycles?'

'No, sir, the *only* book about Nortons.'

'D'you mean to say that in all these years nobody has ever written the history of the most famous name in motorcycling?'

'There have been accounts in magazines and manuals, but this is the first full-length book.'

'Who is writing it?'

'I am.'

'Good luck to you . . . you've a formidable task! The story of 70 years of supremacy . . . it's high time it was told!'

Conversations such as the foregoing came thick and fast when the process of gathering material for these pages was put in hand. First reactions almost invariably expressed astonishment at the realisation that there was no existing work telling the tale of Nortons' fantastic fame. After which came headshaking as appreciation of the magnitude of the undertaking sunk in.

'It could easily run to six volumes,' said one greybeard, as he ran his mind back over the scores of eventful, success-packed years.

'Surely,' he mused, 'since the coming of the petrol engine there's never been a record to surpass it. Norton . . . ' and he savoured the word thoughtfully, 'it's the most famous name in motorcycling.'

Bob Holliday
London, 1972

Preface to Second Edition

WHEN *Norton Story* was first published the amalgamation of Norton Villiers and the BSA-Triumph group was not even mooted. A review of the developments stemming from that marriage brings the present narrative up to 1976 and, as all Norton *aficionados* confidently expect, to the beginning of a new era in the marque's record of continuous motorcycle production through three-quarters of a century.

Comparison of this edition with its predecessor will also reveal changes in the earlier chapters, which have been considerably revised and rearranged; and in this connection I am deeply grateful to 'Pa' Norton's son, Mr J. Lan Norton, CEI, FIMechE, formerly deputy director of design, Rolls-Royce Ltd (Bristol engine division). From his retirement home in Malta, he kindly provided me with much additional material, such as personal family recollections, technical details and factory background, spanning the company's formative years when he assisted his father in establishing Nortons' 'unapproachable' reputation. To his sister, Mrs A. Stocks, of Manchester, I am indebted for the fine portrait of the founder, which appears on page 17.

Certain other facts which have come to light only recently and concern, for example, the real cause of Jimmy Guthrie's fatal accident, and the postponement of the use of the 1937 dohc engines, have been included in the relevant pages.

Bob Holliday
London, December 1975

Acknowledgements

AMONG THE MANY PEOPLE who have been concerned in the preparation of this book I am particularly grateful to the following for variously helping with information, illustrations, encouragement and guidance: Dennis Poore, NVT chairman; Lord Montagu and Michael Ware, National Motor Museum; the late Bill Mansell and Dennis Mansell, Abingdon King Dick Ltd; the editors and staff members of *Motor Cycle* and *Motor Cycle News*; Francis Beart; Nigel Spring; the late John Griffith; C. R. ('Blick') Hodgson; B. R. Nicholls, photographer; Sid Mullarney; Charles Dunne; John Tickle; John Hudson, NV service manager, for verifications; and Joan Power, who did the typing.

Bob Holliday

Chapter 1

Rise . . . and fall

THE OWNER of the surname which has appeared on thousands of tanksides over an era of more than 70 years was James Lansdowne Norton, born in 1869 in the City of Birmingham, England, where he died aged only 56, in 1925, having devoted almost the whole of his working life to designing, developing and perfecting motorcycles that, for mechanical excellence, have always been outstanding.

Jimmie Norton was a clever boy. At the age of 10 he had built a model steam railway engine. To watch it running, large crowds would assemble to peer through the parlour windows of his parents' house—until the police complained that an obstruction of the highway was being caused.

After leaving school he was apprenticed to an engineering toolmaker and later was engaged in the making of bicycle chains.

Then, in 1898, he went into business on his own, forming the Norton Manufacturing Company, mainly to produce fittings and parts for the two-wheel trade. But he already had in mind plans for a petrol-driven bicycle and had done some experimental work when he teamed up, around the turn of the century, with Charles Garrard, importer of French-made Clement engines which sold in Britain under the name Clement-Garrard.

Young Mr Norton's tiny 'works' at 320 Bradford Street, Birmingham, operated as 'manufacturers to the trade', which meant not only assembling Norton motorcycles, mostly custom-built, but also supplying complete machines and parts to other firms creeping into the infant industry.

In 1902 the first 'motorised bicycle' to carry the Norton name had a 1½ hp Clement engine, mounted on the front down tube. There was also a narrow-angle V-twin, while a countershaft two-speed gear and all-chain drive were further refinements later available.

It seems that little machine toolwork was, in fact, done on the Norton premises. Castings, forgings and so forth were 'bought out', and the machining and finishing was shared around the general engineering shops that abounded in Birmingham.

However, all the drive and brain power came from James L. Norton, who presently became so well known and respected for his progressive ideas that other young men engaged in the motorcycle business formed the habit of calling in at Bradford Street for technical natter sessions after business hours, and the office at number 320 became known among them as 'the club'.

With the first half-dozen years of the 20th century gone, Mr Norton still had not produced an engine to his own design, although he had plenty of plans on paper. His lightweight model, called the Energette, now had a small Moto Reve twin-cylinder unit, a Swiss design that was being built in Acton, London. The larger machines had French Peugeot engines—singles and twins with automatic inlet valves.

It was with a privately owned version of the latter type that H. Rem Fowler won the twin-cylinder class of that all-important, first-ever Tourist Trophy race meeting on the Isle of Man in 1907. His achievement played an immense part in consolidating the Norton reputation, for it was a true 'production machine' victory in an event wherein leading contestants were riding factory 'specials' not available to the public.

Rem Fowler who, at the age of 75, was an honoured guest at the Golden Jubilee TT meeting in 1957, was in 1907 a typical Norton private owner. He had purchased his machine direct from Norton's new Floodgate Street works and had competed only in some local hill-climbs with Birmingham and Coventry clubs when he decided to enter for the TT. And, since this was the only Norton machine entered, Jim Norton decided to accompany him.

The TT motorcycle event actually stemmed from the Tourist Trophy car races which had earlier been run in the Isle of Man because there was no speed limit on the island's roads. The Manx government raised no objection when a similar event for motorcycles was suggested, but the course that had been used by the cars, involving a severe mountain climb, was deemed too long and too arduous for the two-wheelers of the time.

Instead, a 15 mile, 1,430 yard triangular circuit on the western side of the Island was chosen. It started in the village of St John's and ran counter-clockwise along the present course from Balla-craine to Kirkmichael, returning, through the

11

FOR HARD WEAR

Holder of 7 WORLD'S RECORDS, 1 mile at 73½ m.p.h. to 150 miles at 64 m.p.h., and winner of innumerable trials—speed, reliability, hill-climbing, flexibility—in all parts of the world.

THE LONG STROKE NORTON with the long, low frame, undoubtedly set the fashion in the motorcycle world. Of scientific design, neat appearance and wonderful capacity power, it has created a remarkable following, "and shows great foresight and grasp of the essential on the part of its designer." —*Press*

"The Unapproachable" NORTON LONG STROKE

General Specification.

Transmission—Big four 1 in. belt, 3½ h.p. ⅞ in. belt. Lyco.

The Tank is of steel, the bottom and sides being formed of one seamless piece (avoiding the bottom joints which are so frequently a source of leakage), heavily tinned, aluminised, and lined in black and red. The rear portion contains the lubricating oil compartment with internal pump just forward of the saddle, so avoiding the long reach and inconvenient stooping position generally necessary when lubricating, and being sheltered, obviates difficulties caused by frozen oil. Capacity—Petrol 1½ gall., Oil ½ gall.

Large Fillers are fitted, enabling the quantity of petrol to be seen at a glance, and the tank to be quickly filled.

Lubrication is by a Tapless pump, through large diameter tubes.

Frame—Is of extremely neat appearance; it gives a very low seat enabling a rider of average height when in the saddle to place both feet firmly upon the ground. The height from ground to top of seat tube is 28½ in.

Footboards—Are of aluminium and of good length with curved up front, very comfortable.

Tyres—2½ in. Clinchers.

Brakes—Norton new non-lock Vee brake, very powerful but sweet in action, and front rim brake.

The Stand—Is of entirely new design, made of stiff tube, oval section and spring operated.

Spring Forks—Special design Norton Druid of graduated width, from wide centre or crown to narrower head and hub, giving great lateral strength to resist sidecar strains.

Saddle—Lyco large, padded pan seat.

Gear—Mark VI., three-speed Armstrong, direct top drive. Gears of 5, 7¼ and 11¼, or varied by a Norton adjustable pulley. Handle or kick starter.

"BIG FOUR" (82 x 120) 636 c.c. For hard pulling, with Sidecar.

3½ h.p. (79 x 100) 490 c.c. FULL TOURING.

NORTON "T.T." 490 c.c. RECORD TYPE.

2½ h.p. (70 x 90) 346 c.c.

The NORTON MANUFACTURING CO. LTD. "The Bridge," Sampson Road North, BIRMINGHAM, ENGLAND.

THE NORTON NEVER BREAKS VALVES.

The Norton Engine of 79 x 100 mm. bore and stroke = 490 c.c. capacity, has too well demonstrated its superiority in design and efficiency to require mention of further proof in so condensed a list. It must suffice to say that the protected features of design, piston and piston rings, with their compression and oil retaining channels are used. The valves are of nickel steel, and 1⅜-in. diameter, and we have yet to record the first breakage of a standard valve head.

Cables: ' NORTOMO, BIRMINGHAM.

This advertisement, printed in a special Overseas Number of Motor Cycling, *dated January 1913, appeared only a few months before the Norton Manufacturing Co Ltd became Norton Motors Ltd. The 2½ hp (70 mm × 90 mm, 346 cc) model listed never materialised.*

streets of Peel, to St John's. The climb of the steep Creg Willey's grade and an awkward S-bend, the Devil's Elbow, were two of its most testing hazards.

To conform with the 'Tourist' title, the event set out to demonstrate and develop not only the reliability but also the economy of motorcycles; so a fuel rationing scheme was introduced.

The great day was Tuesday, May 28, and on a fine, dry morning the 25 starters (17 single-cylinder machines and eight twins) paraded at St John's for the meticulous business of measuring out the petrol. The Class I single-lungers were allowed one gallon for every 90 miles and the Class II twins one gallon for every 75 miles. They had to cover ten laps, a distance of 158¼ miles, and they were started in pairs at one-minute intervals.

Pedalling gear was permitted—and needed, especially on Creg Willey's Hill. Many riders carried spare belts and tubes as well as toolkits. Mid-way through the race there was a ten-minute compulsory 'replenishment and refreshment' stop.

Class I winner, Charlie Collier (Matchless) averaged 38.22 mph and 94½ mpg. Rem Fowler's Norton figures were 36.22 mph and 87 mpg. He made the fastest lap of the day at 42.91 mph. Up to the eighth lap he was leading the field but a burst tyre at the Devil's Elbow caused him to crash at nearly 60 mph. Replacing the butt-ended tube in the beaded-edge cover, without the help of a front prop-stand, cost him 22 minutes delay, and in all he had 13 involuntary stops, one for the tyre, six for mechanical adjustments and six for plug changes.

'Pa' Norton, Rem's only helper, stood at the start frantically waving signals on each lap to pump in more oil—good advice, no doubt, but the occasions when the rider judged it safe to take a hand from the bars to the oil pump were rare indeed!

Since that 1907 event Norton machines have been raced at every TT meeting, a record unapproached by any other make.

With a TT win to spur him on, Jim Norton began producing his own engines. He built singles and twins from 3½ to 5 hp, but he also continued to offer proprietary units such as 2½ hp JAP motors.

At the 1907 Stanley Show he exhibited his Model No 1. Known as the Big Four, it was a long-stroke single of 82 mm × 120 mm, 633 cc, and the type remained in continuous production until the end of 1954 when the company ceased making side-valve engines. A smaller, 82 mm × 90 mm, 475 cc version was also made.

The 1911 TT races saw the introduction of the 500 cc Senior class, and to meet this Norton had an enlarged single-cylinder 79 mm × 100 mm, 490 cc model listed as the '3½', later to become the Model 16 and then the never-to-be-forgotten 16H.

James Norton himself rode one of the new '3½s' in the 1911 TT, which was the first year that the Mountain Course was used. But he was unlucky, as he had been in attempts in the two previous years. In fact, although he was a very keen competition rider, he ought never to have undertaken the rigours of TT contests in three successive years, for he was far from being a fully fit man.

His son, J. Lan Norton, who once helped in designing Nortons before transferring to another branch of engineering, has recorded that: 'During his career my father did not enjoy the best of health—in fact, in his youth, he was discharged from hospital with an incurable heart disease. In the early days of motorcycle manufacture he spent 12 months or so convalescing from an illness in the Isle of Man. It was during this period that the business became somewhat "run down" and was later "rescued" when Mr R. T. Shelley joined the organisation and the name was changed to Norton Motors Ltd.'

But despite illness, and before 'rescue' became necessary, James Norton pressed on enthusiastically. He had moved to premises at Sampson Road North, in Sparkbrook, and there produced, but never marketed, several new models. Among them were a two-stroke Nortonette that weighed only 60 lb and a '2½' (350 cc) version of the '3½'.

The '3½' was already making its mark in speed events. For example, in 1912 Jack Emerson, who later became one of Norton's chief rivals, rode his '3½' from Hull to Brooklands track in Surrey where, although a newcomer to the circuit, he won the 150-mile Brooklands TT, breaking three long-distance world's records in the process!

Nevertheless, in spite of mounting successes, the 'running down' was under way. In 1913, having been engaged right from the start in motorcycle work and having weathered the uncertain, initial years of the industry, the gallant little Norton Manufacturing Company was compelled to liquidate.

Chapter 2

Rescue and revival

IT WAS 'Daddy' Lycett, father-figure in the industry for many years, who arranged the auction of the goodwill and assets of the Norton Manufacturing Company. His saddle-making business, F. W. Lycett Ltd, and R. T. Shelley Ltd, toolmakers who had done machining work for James Norton, were the principal creditors, and at the sale Mr Shelley outbid the only other offer made, so becoming joint managing director, with Mr Norton, of a reconstituted company, Norton Motors Ltd.

Mr C. A. Vandervell, of CAV electrical fame, was chairman of both R. T. Shelley and the new Norton company. His son, Mr Tony Vandervell, world renowned for Vanwall racing cars and shell bearings, was also in later years a Norton chairman.

And now into the picture steps Walter 'Bill' Mansell, who, then in his early twenties, was on the Shelley board, and was also a motorcyclist and a Norton rider. He told me how he acquired the Norton when I called on him at Abingdon King Dick Ltd, one of the several Birmingham companies of which, although over 80, he was then the very active boss.

An early motorcycling friend of his was Percy Evans, then a furniture dealer, who, after winning the 1911 Junior TT on a Humber, turned 'rider-agent' and built up, as P. J. Evans Ltd, one of the biggest motorcycle and car dealerships in the Midlands. In one of his furniture deals Evans found that among the effects, fixtures and fittings he had purchased there was a quite reasonably conditioned Norton motorcycle. This he offered to Bill Mansell, whose two previous machines had not proved satisfactory. 'You can have it,' said PJ, 'for what it stands at on the sales list—£11.'

Bill Mansell, therefore, already had practical Norton experience when Mr Shelley told him to see what could be done to put the new company on a business footing.

It seems that in the Sampson Road North premises all the frame brazing was done on an upper floor, below which was an assembly shop, stores and a separate section for competitions and experimental work. Offices were situated nearby in a considerable area of ground used for trying out machines in a preliminary sort of way. There

was no machine shop, as such. All movable material was transferred to a building in Phillip Street which backed onto Shelleys' Aston Brook Street works. Here there was machinery and equipment that allowed Nortons to make their own engines without having to rely entirely on outside contractors.

Work was concentrated on the 3½ hp (Model 16) and Big Four singles and Mr Norton designed sidecars that were built for him by his friend Tommy Watson, founder of the Watsonian Sidecar company. The Big Four, by the way, was one of the first motorcycles to have integral sidecar lugs. A spring-up rear stand, celluloid-covered handlebars and a tank-top tool box were points that particularly appealed to tourist riders.

For the sporty boys, fast versions of the '3½' TT mount were made and there were also the **BS** and **BRS** models. This remarkable pair, the Brooklands Special and the Brooklands Road Special, were prepared by the original 'Wizard of Tune', D. R. O'Donovan, an Irishman who was a brother-in-law of R. T. Shelley. Having attained fame as a racing cyclist, he took to racing and record-breaking at Brooklands track, where he tuned these special Nortons to such good effect that the **BS** was sold with a guarantee to lap the track at 70 mph—65 mph for the **BRS**. Remember, they were side-valvers with single gear direct belt drive. One owner, who has written lovingly of his **BRS** is Henry Williamson, author of such bewitching books as *Tarka the Otter* and *Salar the Salmon*.

Belt drive was common to all the Nortons, with such optional ancillaries as the Roc two-speed device, the Sturmey-Archer hub gear and the Phillipson variable pulley. For the touring machines the Sturmey-Archer three-speed countershaft gearbox, with either a final belt or all-chain drive, arrived almost concurrently with the outbreak of the First World War in 1914.

With barely a year passed since re-organising, Norton were not in a position, like Douglas in Bristol and Triumph in Coventry, to supply the British Forces with vast quantities of military motorcycles. Their total output for the previous 12 months had not exceeded 100 machines! Nevertheless Bill Mansell made his way to Whitehall and presently gained a contract to supply Big Fours . . . to the Russian government!

For two years there streamed a steady flow of crated solos from Aston to forwarding depots. How many of them ever reached the Russians, and what they did with them, will never be known, for in 1917 came the Red Revolution and, with the Big Bear out of the fight, the shipments ceased and contact with the Czar's army was entirely lost.

Back to the brass-hats went Bill, to be told to carry on producing for the Allies; and the flow of crates ran on unbroken.

Then came November 1918, and the Armistice. This meant no more munitions and machines of

war; petrol went off ration; gratuities were to be spent; there was a huge demand for motorcycles and cars . . . and who is that Birmingham business-man knocking on Whitehall doors? It's Bill Mansell, of course, trying to discover what happens now. What he did eventually find were hundreds of his crated Big Fours, still standing in storage. Practically all the crates were broken open and there were hardly any machines that had not lost magnetos, carburettors, saddles, lamps and horns.

Bill struck a bargain with the authorities, bought back the whole lot and, after a very short period of re-assembly, was supplying an eager civilian market from a stockpile that represented some two years' output of Big Fours.

Chapter 3

Back to business

THE FIRST WORLD WAR ended, so far as actual hostilities were concerned, on November 11 1918—and before the year had expired Norton Motors had prepared a 36-page catalogue.

It was a curious publication. It was not dated and looked very much as though it was the outcome of a cumulative process carried on throughout the war years, there being numerous alterations and additions that suggest it was first intended to cover the 1915/16 range and was changed and up-dated as occasion arose. For instance, illustrated descriptions of the Big Four and Model 16 machines were rubber-stamped 'Cancelled' and a substitute page was stuck in. Included among the 'reading matter' pages were many references to successes in events and letters of tribute from users, none of which was dated later than 1916, the year in which the British Government prohibited the sale of motorcycles for civilian use.

On the back page was glued a red printed notice that is worth reproducing in full:—

NORTON MOTORS LTD, ASTON, BIRMINGHAM NETT PRICES

Subject to alteration without notice

January 1st 1919

Model No		
1	Big 4, chain drive	£87
9	3½ TT*	£63
8	3½ BRS*	£73
7	3½ BS*	£80
16	3½ TT chain drive	£85
	De Luxe Side-car	£28
	Sporting „	£25

* A Phillipson Pulley may be fitted to these models at an extra cost of £5.

Packing in Crates or Cases extra.

Prices above are nett cash ex Works.

So there, in official form, was the first post-Kaiser War Norton range, practically the same as it was in 1914, though the all-belt and chain-cum-belt touring models had been dropped. Note that basically it consisted of five mounts compounded from two types of frame, two sizes of engine and two different forms of gearing transmission.

The Big Four and the Model 16 were almost identical, except for cylinder capacity and total enclosure of the all-chain drive on the former. Both had three-speed, kick-starter Sturmey-Archer gearboxes. Models 7, 8 and 9 shared the same design of frame and forks, and all had belt-drive from the engine shaft. No 7 was a stripped, brakeless, unsilenced record-breaker with a Binks Rat-trap carburettor and a guaranteed 75 mph.

Model 8, guaranteed for 70 mph, had mudguards, tool boxes, front and rear stands, stirrup front and belt-rim rear brakes, and a Brown and Barlow carburettor. The engine, said the catalogue, was 'designed to withstand the excessive strains due to high speeds. In track parlance, "It will not knock itself to bits".'

Though it did not carry the Brooklands speed certificate, the Model 9 TT machine was a replica of the Model 8. All the road-going 490 cc models had a special Norton silencer 'so arranged that any degree of either silence or freedom from exhaust may be obtained'. Owners could 'ride with quietness and decorum to the venue of the competition and there adjust the muffler to give the maximum freedom of exhaust permitted by the judges'.

Tucked away at the back of this circa-1919 brochure are some pages devoted to Competitions and this apparently 'Stop Press' insertion merits re-capping:—

RECORDS

'It will be remembered that our long-standing record of 81.05 miles per hour has been beaten in Switzerland with a speed of 81.5. Brooklands Track was unsafe for speed work owing to War Office lorries having broken it up, nevertheless, a few days after the above event, Mr D. R. O'Donovan took down an *absolutely standard* 490 cc engine, and in spite of the fearfully unsuitable conditions, did *82.85 mph.* This on a pot-holey, undulating surface with a cross wind, and not on a smooth, straight road with a following wind, as we understand was the case in Switzerland. Proving our claim that the Norton is unapproachable for efficiency and power. *We hold 21 World's Class Records.*'

1: *James Lansdowne Norton (1869-1925), whose name first appeared on the tanksides of motorcycles in 1902. The photograph was taken in 1924, Mr Norton's great 'Year of Firsts', when his machines won the Senior and Sidecar TTs and a host of other major events, including the Belgian, French, Spanish and Ulster Grands Prix.*

2: *(Below) Private-owner H. Rem Fowler and James L. Norton (right) at the extemporised 'pits' in readiness for the first-ever Tourist Trophy race in 1907. Rem won the twin-cylinder class at 36.22 mph, setting up the day's fastest lap at 42.91 mph. Nortons have competed at every TT since, a record unapproached by any other make.*

3: (*Above*) *A quintet of satisfied customers meet with the* patron, *Pa Norton (he is standing to the right of the lady in the light coat) at a Birmingham rally, circa 1907-8.*

4: (*Left*) *By 1909 Norton was building his own twin-cylinder engines, having adopted integrally cast automatic inlet valve chests. This well-restored 5 hp 45 degree twin has cylinders of 76 mm × 80 mm, 726 cc.*

5: (*Below*) *Start line scene in the 1910 TT. Competitors pushed off in pairs. Only one Norton took part, ridden by Pa Norton himself, (No. 24) but he failed to finish.*

6: *James Norton astride the machine he rode in the 1909 TT, a newly designed 3½ hp single of 82 mm × 90 mm, 475 cc. Pedalling gear was by then no longer deemed necessary!*

7: *Long wheelbase, long stroke— these were early Norton characteristics. This 1911 Full Touring model had the 79 mm × 100 mm, 490 cc, measurements that distinguished the '500' models for many years.*

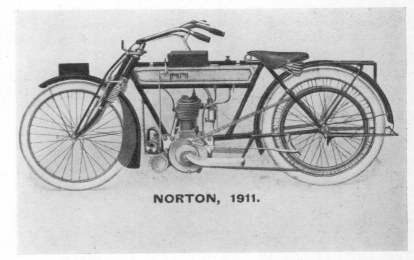

NORTON, 1911.

8: *One of the most famous machines in the National Motor Museum is this 1912 3½ hp flyer, known as 'Old Miracle'. In its time it took more than 100 records, including the flying kilometre in 1915 at 82.85 mph. Note the Binks rat-trap carburettor.*

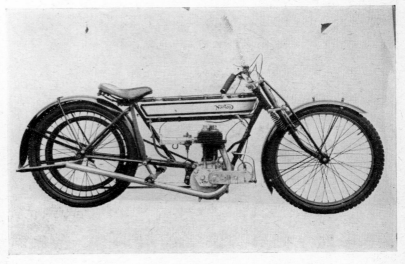

19

79 × 100 - 490 c.c.

9: *Catalogued as a 'sporting model with high speed possibilities', this was the 1915 Tourist Trophy 490 cc machine, carrying the curly 'N' tank transfer. Equipment included a CAV magneto, Brown and Barlow carburettor and, at option, a Phillipson variable gear pulley.*

10: *Stile Kop hill-climb, August 23 1919. Riders 27, 28 and 29 are N. H. Brown (Norton), G. A. (Tony) Vandervell (Norton) and A. D. Draper (Draper-Triumph). J. Smith (Triumph) has his arms folded; No 32 is Graham Walker (Norton) and alongside him is Herbert Le Vack (Edmund-JAP). The officer on the bank is the legendary Major 'Mad Jack' Woodhouse.*

11: (*Above*) *The first ohv Norton to contest the TT was ridden in the 1922 Senior event by Yorkshire's Ralph Cawthorne, seen here on the similar 1923 version, on which he also retired.*

12: (*Right*) *Son of a one-time Norton Motors chairman and later to become world famous for his Vanwall racing cars, Tony Vandervell rode one of the last of the side valve TT Nortons in the 1921 Senior.*

13: (Left) Scottish all-rounder George Grinton raced solos and sidecars in the 1920s. Here he is taking his Norton TT-Hughes outfit round Quarter Bridge to finish fifth in the 1924 Sidecar event. A year later the same machine gained him a third place.

14: (Below) Nortons' first single-cylinder TT win came in 1924—the company's 'Year of Firsts'. Alec Bennett, first rider to raise the race average above 60 mph, is with Bill Mansell, who specially engaged him to do the job.

15: (*Right*) *Just a year before his death James Norton saw his machines win both the Senior and the Sidecar TT races of 1924, the year when Bill Mansell (right) took charge of Bracebridge Street racing plans. Passenger for the victorious George Tucker was Wally Moore, who developed Mr Norton's long-held ohv design and later produced the original Norton ohc engine.*

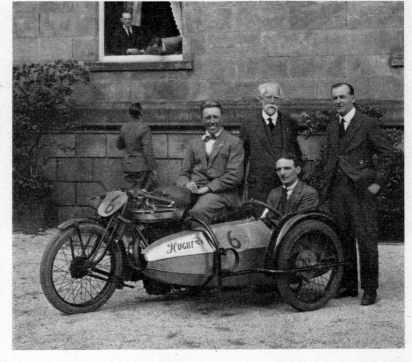

16: (*Below*) *As this 1925 crowd on the hillside shows, Ballig Bridge was once a highly popular TT vantage point, and the flying Norton rider from Spain, I. Macaya, contributes to the day's excitement.*

17: *Who's this prancing along the Quarter Bridge Straight in the early morning? A white number on a dark TT racing plate indicates a practice picture (black numbers on a white ground were used on race days). Spectators on the course means a date prior to 1928, when roads were first closed for training. Actually it's Dubliner Stanley Woods making his first acquaintance with a racing Norton in 1926. The following week it carried him to victory in the Senior event.*

18: *Another Irishman who raced Nortons consistently, often as a factory team member, was Jimmy Shaw from Belfast, seen here on his 1925 Ulster Grand Prix machine.*

'The Unapproachable Norton' slogan had been used in the company's advertisements for several years and may have originated in an 'unsolicited testimonial' stating 'my success is due to my unapproachable Norton'. This anonymous tribute was printed in a 1909 sales leaflet.

In May 1919 it was announced that henceforth Norton intended to make their own sidecar chassis, which had hitherto been 'bought out' for them. Mr. Hubert (Bill) Hassell, the works manager, was responsible for producing Mr Norton's new design.

At the Olympia Show in November three models were displayed, a Big Four and a Model 16 with all-chain drive, and an all-belt '490'. Since it remained successful for so long the Norton sidevalver as it was in 1919 deserves a close look.

The crankcase was notable for its easily cleaned exterior; there were no unnecessary protuberances and no awkward crevices which could harbour dirt. All the cover screws were sunk flush with the case; all corners were radiused and edges rounded.

An unusually large oil sump allowed a greater-than-normal amount of lubricant to be held in reserve for hill-climbing and speed bursts. Lubrication was, of course, of the constant-loss type, oil being fed from the tank by drip feed or direct hand pump.

To prevent drumming or springing, the interior of the timing case was ribbed and the external faces of the cams were half an inch wide, as were the lever-type followers.

The Big Four had flywheels 8¼ inches in diameter and 1½ inches wide. After mounting on their shafts the flywheels were ground to ensure complete accuracy. Main shafts had roller bearings on the drive side and ball bearings on the timing side. Shafts were of low carbon steel, case-hardened and ground.

With its square, four-stud base, the one-piece cylinder was a splendid casting, deeply finned and with air spaces between the valve chamber and the barrel. The overall appearance of the Norton side valve engines changed little in a long life, even after they had acquired enclosed springs and detachable heads. Indeed, the crankcase served equally well when overhead valves arrived.

Up to 1919 the connecting rod had phosphor-bronze bushed big and little ends, with a two-ring cast-iron piston held by split pins on the hollow gudgeon pin; 490 cc models had domed piston crowns—the Big Four's was flat.

It was with these simple, sturdy engines that 'Wizard' O'Donovan obtained his records and produced his Brooklands certificates. Exactly how

it was done Nortons were not prepared to reveal. 'We are frequently asked,' they said, 'the difference between the standard TT engine, which *may* develop record speeds, and the BS, which does and *will* attain record speeds. This is our secret; the difference is the reason for the speed, and we must ask our friends to accept the speed as the difference.'

On completion at the works these special engines were sent in batches to Brooklands where, after a few preliminary laps, they were timed by an official of the Brooklands Automobile Racing Club over the kilometre—or over a lap—and a certificate was then issued recording that an individual unit had exceeded the stipulated speed. It was stressed that the speed certified—75 mph, for example—did not represent the limit, or even the speed attained by that particular unit, but merely that the speed which Nortons guaranteed for all Brooklands engines of that type had officially been *exceeded* during test.

Afterwards the unit, exactly as when certified, was transferred to its frame and, after passing a short road test, was ready for despatch.

Notice that it was the engine—not the complete motorcycle—that was speed tested. For example, for the track gallop each unit was fitted into one of the engine-less machines O'Donovan maintained at Weybridge for this purpose.

A typical Brooklands Test Certificate read as follows:—

BROOKLANDS AUTOMOBILE RACING CLUB

I certify that the Norton Motor Cycle Engine No. 201133 Make of Engine—Norton No. of Cylinders—one: has exceeded a speed of 75 miles per hour for a Kilometre on Brooklands Motor Track.

Dated 22nd day of January, 1921
F. H. Rance, Superintendent.

Note: A Kilometre=1094 yards.

But it was not only the BS engines that got exhaustive testing. All production machines were first run under their own power in a test frame. If this proved satisfactory, each was then given a road test for power, flexibility, hill-climbing, handling, and so forth and the results were recorded on a test card. The engine was then taken to pieces, each part examined and, subject to everything being in order, it was re-assembled, fitted to its machine, and taken for a final road test.

Chapter 4

Bracebridge Street

WITH TWENTY YEARS of production exclusively devoted to motorcycles behind them, Nortons moved into the 1920s on a wave of enthusiasm for the sport. And they also moved to a new address that was to become as renowned as the Norton name itself—Bracebridge Street.

The story of how this change came about was told to me by Bill Mansell. He was in the habit of taking his lunch at the old Royal Hotel in Temple Row, Birmingham, and one of his table companions was Mr J. Goodman, father of Percy and Eugene Goodman, all three of whom were engaged in laying the foundations of the Velocette reputation. Though in a way rival manufacturers, Mansell and Goodman were on the friendliest of terms, and one day Mr Goodman remarked that he was thinking of shifting the Veloce factory from its Fleet Street site in Birmingham's city centre to bigger premises. After lunch he was going to inspect a place that sounded suitable, and he asked if Bill would care to come with him. To his astonishment, Mr Bill was taken to Bracebridge Street to look at a row of buildings which practically backed on to his own works at Phillip Street, yet no one at Nortons knew they were vacant!

Bill Mansell waited a week and then telephoned Mr Goodman to ask if he had taken any decision. 'The boys want to move out of the city centre,' he was told. 'They've settled on Six Ways, Aston.' They did, in fact, move to that site, and later became thorns in Nortons' racing side for years.

The Bracebridge Street buildings had housed a firm called Laws Ash, makers of wire netting, and the place was full of machinery intended for that purpose. Bill had it all smashed up and taken away, and Nortons moved in to settle down to a run of occupancy that lasted until 1963.

No one could ever have called its low, brick-built frontage an impressive facade in keeping with the fame it acquired but, in those 43 years, narrow, shabby Bracebridge Street saw the comings and goings of motorcycling's mightiest men. In his new surroundings Pa Norton started to develop some of the ideas he had not been able to put into practice while the company was on war production. Plans for a 350 cc engine had to be put on one side, but he changed the long-favoured plain big-end to a set of rollers running directly on the crankpin in a tapered H-section connecting rod drilled from eye to eye.

Naturally he had his eye on the Isle of Man, for 1920 saw the resumption of TT racing after the war break—and a Norton success was badly needed. Since Rem Fowler's twin-cylinder victory in 1907 the company's record in Manxland had been pretty grim. A 10th place in 1908 and 46th and 51st in 1914 was all they had achieved, though they had supported the event every year.

Clearly something better was expected from a marque that claimed 21 world's records and successes in other races, hill-climbs, trials, etc.

As it happened, the 1920 Senior Tourist Trophy eluded them by only $3\frac{1}{2}$ seconds. Their chief and most experienced protagonist, Manxman Douggie Brown, who had ridden in every TT meeting since 1910 and was on a Norton for the first time, went into furious battle with the formidable Sunbeam team and, in one of the hardest fought races yet seen, 10 of the 18 finishers were Norton mounted.

Encouraged by such a promising beginning to post-war racing, Norton returned to the Island in 1921 with a strong force of riders, works entries including Douggie Brown, Victor Horsman, J. W. (Jimmy) Shaw, Bill Hassall, and the son of the company's chairman, Tony Vandervell. But their high hopes came crashing down. One after another the giants fell out and from 16 Norton starters only three survived, the best performance, sixth place, being made by J. L. Mitchell, a private owner.

Despite this Manx disaster the Norton reputation continued high and was spreading throughout the world. At Brooklands Rex Judd, a dark-haired, tough little 18-year-old jockey from O'Donovan's stable, riding a $3\frac{1}{2}$ hp side valve BS model, raised the 500 cc two-way kilometre record to 86.37 mph.

At the Show a new model, called the Colonial, was introduced, with a crankcase clearance of 6 inches. The standard $3\frac{1}{2}$ hp model now became the 16H, with a lower riding position and the transverse, can-shaped silencer below the magneto. The Model 9 Super Speedster belt-driven machine, a development of the BRS, was shown at Olympia and the Big Four was offered with Lucas Magdyno electric lighting at £21 extra.

Chapter 5

The ohv Norton

ON MARCH 15 1922 the Brooklands season opened with the first appearance in public of a long-standing 'open secret', the overhead valve Norton —cautiously announced as 'for experimental purposes only; not on the market'.

By this time ohv engines were nothing new; indeed, there were already several well-established overhead camshaft designs, among them being the Sunbeams ridden so outstandingly by George Dance. Two years earlier a Norton private owner, Ralph Cawthorne, had had some success in speed trials with an ohv conversion of his own devising.

Pa Norton's somewhat tardy 'experiment' was therefore watched with great interest when Rex Judd wheeled it out of O'Donovan's Brooklands shed for a crack at world's records. Observers noted that, except for the part of the engine above the crankcase, the machine was pretty much the same as the side-valver on which Judd had set records in the previous year. The 79 mm × 100 mm, 490 cc cylinder carried on its head a pair of standards supporting rockers operated by parallel, vertical push-rods. A single tension spring linked the rockers to return the rods. A large, circular, finned nut held the left-side exhaust pipe to the cylinder head and a Binks Rat-trap carburettor was fitted.

Rex gave rival spies little chance to see much more of his machine. After he had raised the 500 cc kilometre record to 89.92 mph, and the mile to 88.39 mph, the model was hustled into O'Donovan's tuneshop and did not reappear in the public eye until TT practising began in the summer.

Norton factory entries for the 1922 Senior Race were Douggie Brown, Bill Hassall, Norman Black and Jimmy Shaw, all on side-valvers, and R. T. Cawthorne on an ohv. Among some nine private entries were George Tucker, Vic Horsman, Tommy Simister (side valves) and Tony Vandervell (ohv).

In fact, Vandervell withdrew and Norton competition manager Graham Walker—who was not in the original entry list, but was in charge of the private owners' camp—took over Tony's entry, practising on the ohv. But when it came to Senior Day, Graham, who had raced Nortons in 1920 and 1921, elected to use a side valve model, leaving

R. T. Cawthorne as the only remaining ohv rider.

It had not been an easy practising period for the Norton boys. Midway through the session it had been decided to change the aluminium pistons to cast-iron ones, and this had involved much overtime spent on balancing flywheel assemblies.

Nor was Senior Day without its troubles. Best Norton performance was made by Graham Walker, who finished fifth; next best was a veteran private owner, J. W. Adamson, in tenth berth. Nine of the 14 Norton starters failed to finish, including Cawthorne who went out on the last lap when lying 15th, 'every kind of trouble', according to a contemporary report, 'having beset the largely experimental ohv'.

Nevertheless, James Norton learned from experience, and when the Model 18 490 cc ohv Norton was introduced as a road-going machine at the Olympia Show—at £98—it was seen that a number of changes had been made. The overhead valve gear had been rearranged, shortening the overall height of the engine. The original cast bronze rocker standards were replaced by steel forgings and a new type of slipper piston was used. Return springs were fitted at the bases of the push-rods and a lower, shorter frame had been devised. An internal expanding drum brake was on the front hub and there was a dummy belt rim brake at the rear. With its sweeping, left-side exhaust pipe ending in a tubular silencer it was a rakish, exciting-looking motorcycle, destined to send Norton's racing reputation rocketing and to become one of the best-loved sports machines ever made.

Companions to the Model 18 at the Olympia Show were the 16H and Big Four models with redesigned combustion chambers and lubrication systems, and the Model 9 made its final appearance—the last direct belt-drive machine of over 350 cc to be marketed.

Two months before the Show it had been announced that Norton had on the stocks an ohv 250 cc (63 mm × 80 mm) engine, with the magneto mounted behind the cylinder, but this never appeared; in fact, over 30 years were to pass before Bracebridge Street offered a quarter-litre model— the parallel-twin Jubilee.

Having at last abandoned the side-valvers for racing, Norton went to the 1923 TT with an all-ohv string of machines claimed to be completely standard with no special gadgets. The Senior entries comprised Graham Walker, Jimmy Shaw, Norman Black, Graeme Black, Tom Simister, Bill Hassall and R. T. Cawthorne. Graham Walker and George Tucker contested the first-ever Sidecar Race with 588 cc engines.

In both races the Trophies just escaped Norton riders. In the Sidecar event Walker and Tucker were second and third behind Freddie Dixon's banking Douglas outfit. In the Senior it was Edinburgh's Graeme Black who gave principal chase to the ultimate winner, Manxman Tommy Sheard (Douglas). Despite a stop to adjust brakes ('compensation for unfair wear and tear,' he said), a tumble at Creg-ny-Baa, and no pit signalling system, Graeme came a gallant second and, with Walker (fourth) and Simister (fifth), won for Nortons their first Manufacturers' Team Prize.

Evidently the troubles that had beset the 1922 ohv had been eliminated and when, in the following September, the Manx Motor Cycle Club ran the first 'Amateur TT'—officially called the Amateur Road Race Championship—push-rod Nortons again came close to victory. R. O. Lowe and G. Bower were leading the field on the penultimate lap; then Lowe fell, after having made the day's fastest lap, and Bower's engine gave up at the Bungalow when he was ahead with three minutes in hand over the eventual winner, L. H. Randles (Sunbeam). Bower coasted and pushed home to finish 11th.

Pa Norton was much interested in seeing for himself the export potential for his machines, and he had set out in 1921 on an extensive tour of South Africa, using a high-ground-clearance Big Four sidecar outfit. It was an exhaustive and, for a man in frail health, exhausting, exercise, but he returned in 1922 full of ideas for adapting the Colonial models even better to suit overseas conditions.

At the Show in October, two ohv models were exhibited, the standard Model 18 roadster and a version with full TT equipment, including a large-capacity fuel tank and a separate oil tank on the saddle tube. The crankcase rockers had roller cam followers and double-row caged roller bearings were fitted in the overhead rockers. The machines still had dummy belt rim rear brakes.

If Nortons had no Tourist Trophy to display they had other prizes of which they could be proud. One was a certificate to show that, on October 4th, a few days before Show opening, Albert Denly, riding one of O'Donovan's specially tuned machines at Brooklands, had taken the much coveted Hour record, averaging 85.22 mph. (See Chapter 23.)

Also occupying a prominent place on the stand was the handsome, newly introduced Maudes Trophy—awarded for 'the most meritorious performance of the year in an ACU observed trial'. (See Chapter 8.)

Chapter 6

A Year of Firsts

1924 WAS a bonanza year. After a quarter of a century of ups and downs in fortune, Norton enjoyed a season of such outstanding, sustained success in all branches of the sport that, at the end of it, the company published a booklet entitled 'A Year of Firsts'.

To get the picture in proper perspective it should be borne in mind that up to this juncture Norton policy had been based on two main precepts: (1) to make good motorcycles for the general public, and (2) to demonstrate their qualities by ensuring, so far as was reasonably possible, that all the mounts they entered in competitions were strictly 'as you can buy', ridden for the most part by enthusiastic private owners and dealers, some of whom would be 'works-supported' to team up with one or two of the Bracebridge Street staff. A TT outing was a sort of happy-family affair, with Pa looking after a group of boys all about equally good as all-round riders and all using machines that were pretty well identical. There were no special stars and no special gadgets.

Early in 1924 Bill Mansell took a hard look at this situation and decided that if the company was to get to the top in this racing business the job had better be tackled in a more business-like manner. He was convinced that in the Model 18 there was a potential winner and he argued (with himself only) that the safest way to ensure victory was to put it in the hands of the man who everyone said was most likely to win.

He picked up his telephone and put through a call to Alec Bennett.

Mr Bill told me that the conversation went like this:

'That you, Alec? I'd like to come down to Southampton and discuss a little matter with you.'

'I think I know what it is. I haven't yet fixed anything for the Senior, but I'd be glad to.'

'What about terms, agreements, and so on?'

'Oh, I'll leave all that to you, Bill. I'm sure it will be a fair deal.'

And, of course, it was.

To support Alec in the Senior, works entries were made for that trio of stalwarts, Bill Hassall, Graeme Black and Tommy Simister. Right from the earliest days there had existed a strong affinity between Norton and Ireland—stemming probably from Dan O'Donovan's influence—so there was also a semi-official team from Ulster consisting of Belfast dealer Jimmy Shaw, and a couple of new boys called J. F. Dinsmore and Joe Craig. Coventry dealer W. J. 'Billy' Lord, J. A. Stuart and South African H. B. Loader made up the solo contingent.

There were only two Nortons in the sidecar race, both 588 cc jobs, works entered and driven by Bristolian George Tucker and Scotsman George Grinton.

In the spring of 1924 the technical magazines had heralded 350 cc—and even 250 cc—TT Nortons but nothing was seen of them. Nor did anything come of a patent lodged by J.L.N. for an overhead camshaft design in which the springless valves were operated by rockers controlled from 'grooved cams cut in the face of a rotary member revolving in a vertical plane, driven by chain from the engine shaft, each rocker having a pin which fits into the grove, the other end working in a slot cut in the valve stem'. The system was described as 'desmodromique'.

On practice form the Sidecar race looked like being a four-pronged battle between the two Norton 588s and the 600 cc Douglases of Freddie Dixon and Alfie Alexander. As it happened, neither of the Douggies survived two of the four laps and Tucker, whose passenger was another Bristolian, one Walter Moore, beat the second man, Harry Reed, on a 350 cc Dot, by nearly half an hour!

A walkover it may have been, but it brought Nortons their first-ever Trophy, for Rem Fowler's prize in 1907 was a silver rose bowl—which, by the way, he never received!

The Senior race was clearly going to be a single versus twin affair, for there were strong entries from Scott and Douglas. That it would be an exceptionally fast race was certain for several riders had approached mile-a-minute laps during the practice period.

Chief threat for Norton was again Fred Dixon, and the man from Middlesbrough took the lead right away, hurling his Douglas into a record lap of 63.75 mph and holding first berth on lap after lap. But the level-headed Bennett, aided by efficient pit signalling, knew exactly what he was doing. He said after the race that he had seldom exceeded three-quarter throttle, saving himself for the last of the six laps. When he caught up with Dixon in Ramsey he knew he was all right and when his winning engine went through the post-race technical examination it was found to be in well-nigh perfect condition. As with all the other Nortons it had an absolutely standard specification; the alloy slipper piston ran on a compression ratio of 5.1:1—'suitable for ordinary BP spirit'.

The four other Norton finishers were Hassall (5th), Stuart (9th), Loader (10th) and Craig (12th).

For the first time a TT race had been won at over 60 mph—Alec's average was 61.64 mph. Second and third place men Harry Langman (Scott) and Dixon also bettered '60' and 11 men exceeded the 1923 winning speed. Mr Norton attended the races and was loudly cheered when he supported the Irish-Canadian Alec Bennett at the prize distribution.

At a civic dinner party given by the Birmingham Corporation in honour of the city's two doubly successful motorcycle factories (the Twemlow brothers, Kenneth and Eddie, had won the Junior and Lightweight races for New Imperial), James Norton said he had waited 19 years for that night!

At the Olympia Show in October there were over 80 individual motorcycle and three-wheeler makers displaying their wares. On the Norton stand there were no major model changes to be seen, but the array of awards won in that Year of Firsts was dazzling to behold.

For the record, Norton motorcycles had in 1924 finished *first* in each of the following international events:—

Senior TT
Sidecar TT
Belgian GP (500 class)
French GP (500 class)
Spanish GP
Spanish 24-hour race
Italian Circuit de Cremona
Scottish Championships (500 class)
Irish Championships (500 class)
Tailtean Races (Dublin)
Welsh TT (500 class)
Brooklands 200-mile sidecar race (also second, third, fourth and fifth)
Brooklands 200-mile solo race (500 class)
Leinster 100
Ulster GP (500 class: also second, third and fourth)

In other spheres of racing Norton riders had also won 32 hill-climbs, 39 speed trials and 52 beach races—123 victories; the next best marque was Douglas with 85 firsts. At Brooklands Norton solos and sidecars had notched up a host of time and distance records, outstanding among which was Bert Denly's 83.93 mph for 200 solo miles. Endurance and reliability events had netted cups and medals galore and, for the second year running, the Maudes Trophy graced the Show stand.

No wonder those whose tanksides carried the curly 'N' Norton insignia rode their mounts with a special air of pride!

Chapter 7

The mid-'Twenties

IF THE SILVER, red and black Norton colours had flown proudly over Bracebridge Street through 1924, the following year saw them lowered to half mast for, on April 21 1925, at the age of 56 after a long and painful illness, James Lansdowne Norton passed away at his home in Sampson Road, Birmingham.

I did not have a chance to meet Mr Norton, for I had only just left school when he died. In later years I listened to many of his contemporaries—including Rem Fowler, Bill Mansell and Joe Craig—extolling his qualities both as a man and as an engineer, but I cannot myself pay a just tribute to someone I never knew. Instead, I will quote one of motorcycling's most esteemed historians, the late Jim Sheldon, who in a 1957 Golden Jubilee TT issue of *Motor Cycling* wrote of J.L.N. as follows:—

'He was a very religious man, a leading figure in the Salvation Army in Birmingham, and his motorcycles seemed to reflect his whole attitude to life. It was more than a trite "putting the best into them". He put everything he had into them and in the end had the rest of the world following him.'

Only a few months before his death Mr Norton, having for health reasons resigned the presidency of the British Motor Cycle and Cycle Research Association, had been elected its first honorary member. In his memory the Norton Scholarship in Motorcycle Engineering at Birmingham University was instituted after a fund had been raised to which contributions came from all over the world.

In the field of road racing that year the firm struck a dull patch—another of those 'nearly but not quite' spells that had plagued them up to the Year of Firsts.

For the 1925 TT reliance was placed on a stable of mounts not much altered in appearance or overall specification. Mechanical detail changes included the fitting of a double plunger oil pump mounted below the timing case to provide a dry-sump lubrication system, and the overhead valve gear was modified to take longer springs. Ball-ends on the rocker arms fitted into cups on the tops of the push-rods. In this year Sunbeam were using hairpin valve springs and Velocette entered the Junior Race with an ohc mount that Geoff Povey had already ridden experimentally in reliability trials.

The three Nortons in the Sidecar race were 588s in the hands of A. E. Taylor and the two Georges, Grinton and Tucker. The Douglas company got its own back with Len Parker's victory and Freddie Dixon's fastest lap at 57.18 mph. Taylor and Grinton were second and third, Tucker having dropped out on the fourth and last lap. Only eight of the 14 starters finished in this, the last of the three Sidecar TTs of the 1920s.

The Nortons in the Senior event were headed by Alec Bennett, Tom Simister and Joe Craig. With the Bracebridge Street boys for the first time was Ernie Searle, who had previously ridden Sheffield-Henderson and Douglas machines, and among the 'foreign field' were a couple of Spanish Norton private owners, J. Vidal and I. Macaya; the latter, being left-handed, had all his handlebar controls 'reversed'.

Alec Bennett opened up with a record lap in 33 min 50 sec, forging well ahead of the opposition, which consisted of the very swift AJS models and the new JAP-engined HRD ridden by its manufacturer, Howard Davies.

With a comfortable lead, Bennett was just about to complete his second lap when a patch of oil on the road at Governor's Bridge caused a tumble that bent a foot rest in such a way that it stuck into the ground on right-hand turns.

The spill had let Howard Davies into the lead and relegated Bennett to sixth place. Joe Craig battled manfully in second berth for four laps before retiring in favour of Frank Longman (AJS). Bennett had worked his way back through the field and finished third.

Nortons introduced at the Show a new four-speed gearbox designed and made by themselves to supplement the three-speed Sturmey-Archer component. Control was by a quadrant lever on the tankside. Constant mesh pinions on roller bearing shafts were used and the kick-starter mechanism was all-enclosed. The box was fitted to the Big Four and also to a new 588 cc ohv model with a specification otherwise similar to that of the 490 cc ohv. All the ohv models were equipped with enclosed front chaincases and Webb-type forks—except the 588 which had Druid forks. The 3½ hp side valve 16H was at last provided with a rear hub brake.

A 490 ohv solo and a 588 ohv sidecar outfit had successfully completed a rigorous observed test, again winning the Maudes Trophy. At the Brooklands circuit the record-breakers had had another busy season.

At the start of practising for the 1926 TT an Isle of Man paper noted that Mr W. Mansell and Mr Walter Moore, of Nortons, were staying at the Castle Mona Hotel. Wally Moore, who had earlier had much to do with the development of Douglas engines, had joined the Bracebridge Street team after he had passengered for George Tucker in the 1924 Sidecar TT. Other recruits to the factory, with a special interest in the experimental department, were Joe Craig and record-breaker C. W. G. (Bill) Lacey.

However, not much change had been made to the 6.4 : 1 compression ratio Norton engines for this, the first seven-lap meeting. The oil pump had been revised and was supplied from a rather ugly-looking container mounted above the fuel tank on the top tube.

But if the technical side had remained static, Bill Mansell had been at it again in the human relations department. A Dublin dealer-friend, perhaps a bit nettled that so many of Norton's Irish riders had hailed from Ulster, said 'Why don't you give one of our boys a chance? On a Norton there's a sure winner in young Stanley Woods'.

Stanley was then 22 years of age. He had made his TT debut when 18 and had finished fifth on a Cotton in the 1922 Junior event. On the same make in the next year he had won the Junior Trophy. In six other Island races up to 1925 he had variously ridden Cotton, Scott, New Imperial and Royal Enfield—and retired every time. On paper it looked as if Irish luck was fickle for the young

Dubliner. Nevertheless, the invitation to join the Norton team went forth.

While Stanley was getting to know his Norton during the practising his Senior (in both senses) team-mate Bennett was away on the Continent winning the French Grand Prix in the teeth of mighty opposition from the indigenous Peugeots— vertical twin ohc machines of great potency.

Alec returned to the Island in time to make his qualifying laps and on the Monday he easily won the Junior Trophy with a Velocette. But in the Big Race his Norton went sour, clutch trouble eliminating him very early on. For two laps there was no one in the picture except the meteoric Jimmy Simpson who drove his AJS to an over-70 mph lap record before something drastic happened to it. Thereupon the new-to-Nortons Stanley stepped into the lead and beat second place man Walter Handley by over four minutes at the record race speed of 67.54 mph. Handley was riding a V-twin Blackburne-engined Rex-Acme, a marque he used in 14 TT races. In 12 years of Island racing he used eight different makes of motorcycle in 28 races and the only time he ever started on a Norton was in the Junior of 1934, when he retired.

Of the five Norton entries in the 1926 Senior, three finished the course. The ever-present Joe Craig was fourth behind Frank Longman (AJS) and the cack-handed Spaniard Macayo was 11th.

There were no Show surprises but, in addition to the Senior Trophy and the French Grand Prix, the Norton stand displayed, for the fourth successive year, the Maudes Trophy, captured after another convincing demonstration of road-going reliability.

During the year, as a consequence of financial restructuring, the company altered its name to Norton Motors (1926) Ltd.

Chapter 8

The Maudes Trophy

WE'LL TAKE A BREAK NOW, from the continuing story of Norton development, and have a good look at something that has persistently popped up since 1923—the Maudes Trophy. What was it—and why was it considered to be so important? Also, how come Nortons appeared to have such a perennial grip on it?

To find answers to those questions we need to go back not just to 1923 but to the period 20 years earlier when, for the first time, the motorcycle movement was being knitted together under the guidance and control of one democratically elected representative body—the organisation we have known for so long as the Auto-Cycle Union.

The ACU (at first it was called Auto-Cycle Club) began with a portfolio of aims and objects—like listing approved hotels, fixing cheap railway fares for broken-down machines, arranging cut-price insurance, fighting anti-motorcycle legislation and so forth. But its main task was to bring order into the world of motorcycle sport. At that time all sorts of impressarios and entrepreneurs were running advertising stunts, unofficial tests and so-called records. The general public, from the start hostile towards 'those noisy motor-bicycles', was becoming increasingly dubious about the authenticity of the extravagant claims that were being made for economy, speed and reliability.

The ACU tackled the problem in two main ways. It drew up for all its constituent clubs a set of rules governing the running of motorcycle contests; and it established a headquarters competitions committee and department responsible for appointing official timekeepers and measurers, observing and certifying record attempts and special tests, as well as organising ACU-sponsored events designed to demonstrate the general all-round usefulness of motorcycles. Out of this, as every schoolboy knows, came the Tourist Trophy Race, an event originally intended, as its name suggested, to show how economically, speedily and reliably an ordinary touring machine could perform.

Fifty years after he had won the twin-cylinder class in the first-ever TT in 1907, Rem Fowler told me that when he decided to enter his privately owned Norton in the event he hardly gave a thought to the speed aspect of the contest. And

when he took his mount round to the Norton works to have it overhauled for the event, 'Pa' Norton's main consideration was to ensure that it was capable of covering the race distance on the quantity of petrol allowed by the regulations. Chief endeavours to provide reliability (ie, finishing the race at all costs) took the form of equipping the rider with as much breakdown kit as he could carry, including spare inner tubes, driving belts, sparking plugs, valve springs, tyre levers and pump, and enough tools to deal with almost every nut, bolt, stud and screw on the machine.

Petrol limitations in the TT lasted for only two years. In 1909 the event had become a straight road race with the accent entirely on speed. Even silencers, hitherto compulsory fittings in the interests of 'touring', had been abandoned.

This concentration on out-and-out speed stepped up after the Great War—and there were quite a lot of people who didn't care too much for the way things were going. Everywhere there were road races, hill-climbs, sprints, beach events and Brooklands—all of them becoming faster and faster.

Mr George Pettyt, of Maudes Motor Mart, Exeter, was one of those who thought it was about time to emphasise that motorcycles could do more than rush around at high velocity and that there were plenty of good machines besides those that won TTs.

Mr Pettyt's idea was to present the ACU with a very handsome and valuable silver vase, called at first the Pettyt Cup and later the Maudes Trophy, which was to be used to encourage motorcycle manufacturers to undertake worthwhile and public demonstrations of their products under strict, impartial observation. The trophy was to be awarded annually to the firm whose observed and certified test was considered by the ACU to be the year's most meritorious effort.

From its inception in 1923, and right through the 1930s, there were many epic attempts to win the Maudes and some amazingly difficult and laborious special endeavours were devised and carried through. The donor's object in providing something that would stress the stamina of standard products, as opposed to the TT emphasis on the speed of special machines, caught the imagination of the industry and gained the ap-

33

proval of an interested British motorcycling public.

The concept behind the Maudes Trophy tallied exactly with James Norton's own precepts. From his early days as a motorcycle maker he had preached and practised the gospel of using standard production machines for competition work. Time and again his catalogues and advertisements had sought to impress that factory-entered Nortons in races and other competitive events were genuine 'as-you-can-buy' machines without gimmickry or special effects. Now the conditions governing the award of the Maudes Trophy gave him a chance to prove his claims and Norton was the first company to enter the contest.

One would have thought that the obvious machine to use for such a competition would be the Big Four, or perhaps the 16H, for the Norton reputation for reliability had been built up by those sturdy side-valvers. But no; James Norton decided that what was needed was indisputable proof of the dependability of his comparatively new machine, the 490 cc overhead valve Model 18. And since this was a mount intended for speed work, a speed test it should have—despite any other preconceived ideas about the purpose of the Maudes Trophy!

So, on September 13 1923, an ACU official visited the Norton works and selected from stock the parts of an ohv engine. Piston, rocker arms, cylinder, crankcase and flywheels were stamped by him and the engine was assembled under his supervision. Without any kind of testing the unit was taken to O'Donovan's Brooklands workshop and fitted into a standard frame—all under ACU observation. The complete machine was then run over 29 laps of the $2\frac{3}{4}$-mile circuit, after which two adjustments were made—slight easing of the piston to increase the clearance above the top ring, and re-timing of the standard CAV magneto which was also selected from stock.

The machine then started on a 12-hour run, ridden in stints by O'Donovan, Nigel Spring and Albert Denly. During the 12 hours the following 18 world's records were broken in Class C (500 cc solo) and Class D (750 cc solo):—

7, 8, 9, 10, 11 and 12 hours; 500, 600 and 700 miles. Speeds ranged between 63.79 mph for the seven hours and 64.02 mph for the 700 miles.

On being dismantled the engine was found to be in perfect condition; the ACU reckoned that Jim Norton had proved his point and awarded him the Maudes Trophy.

Over the next three years Norton entries for the Maudes award were almost entirely angled on road-going reliability, and in all three cases a lead-

ing part was played by Phil Pike, of Plymouth.

This West Country Norton dealer was, like so many riders of the period, a real all-rounder, equally adept with solo or sidecar in any kind of competition, from racing to trials. He rode in every TT meeting from 1914 to 1926, in which latter year he was also the Norton sidecar-driving member of the team which won the International Six Days Trial for Britain.

Pike's task for the 1924 Maudes attempt was to drive a Big Four combination, assembled under ACU observation from stock parts, from Land's End to John o' Groats and repeat the performance, making four end-to-end journeys in all. It was intended to maintain a 20 mph average speed over the 4,000 miles involved. This had almost been achieved when, at approximately 3,500 miles, the outfit was run into and badly damaged by a motor coach. Repairs, using stock parts and components taken from a local Norton agent's store, upset the running average, but Pike completed the schedule and then went on to make 20 consecutive climbs of Porlock Hill, the last one at over 21 mph.

Petrol consumed for the 4,083-mile journey worked out at 68.4 mpg, and the total weight of the outfit, including the crew's luggage, was 8 cwt 4 lb.

Pike's passenger for this, and the two following Maudes adventures, was the ACU's engineer, Arthur B. Bourne, who subsequently became, for a quarter of a century, editor of *The Motor Cycle*.

A plan to cover four classic long-distance test routes in quick succession was made for the 1925 Maudes entry. The two machines, a 490 cc ohv solo and a 588 cc ohv sidecar outfit, were, as before, built up from stock parts under observation. Then, with Arthur Bourne in Pike's sidecar and Bill Hassall on the solo, the party set off to follow the Motor Cycling Club's London-Exeter route, maintaining a 20 mph schedule as if actually under trials conditions. From Exeter the London-Land's End route, including Porlock, Lynton and Beggars' Roost hills, was taken and from 'the End' the machines turned north to John o' Groats after which the MCC's London-Edinburgh trial hills were conquered.

The test started on August 31 and finished at Brooklands on September 15, the total distance being 3,183 miles, during which the solo averaged 112.1 mpg and the combination 81.1 mpg. On reaching the Weybridge track both machines were given high-speed runs. Told to lap at 60 mph, Hassall did 61.5; Pike, aiming at 50, achieved 53.4 mph. A little later, still under ACU control, and after a few minor adjustments to chains, tappets, tyre pressures and so on, both Nortons went out on a 12-hour record attack. In those 12 hours, with Hassall, Pike, O'Donovan and Denly riding, no fewer than 32 long-distance world's records were broken.

The fourth Maudes venture differed essentially from the others in that the machine used was not built up from ACU chosen parts—nor was it even a new model. In fact, it was Phil Pike's own ride-to-work 588 cc ohv with a sports sidecar. During the summer of 1926, with that celebrated Devonian motoring medico Dr G. H. S. Letchworth in the 'chair', Pike had driven this outfit as a member of the victorious British team in the International Six Days Trial, held that year in the Peak District.

After the trial the outfit was driven with an ACU observer-passenger to a garage at Weybridge, where it was sealed and locked up. Three weeks later Phil Pike and Arthur Bourne wheeled it from the lock-up, started it at first kick, and with no more attention than tank topping, drove to Dinas Mawddy in mid-Wales.

Just a few miles beyond Dinas is Bwlch-y-Groes, the 'Pass of the Cross', which runs over the edge of Snowdonia down into Bala. A mile and a half long, rising to 1,140 feet with an average gradient of 1 in 7 and a 1 in 4 hairpin section, it was regarded as a real 'terror'. Pike's objective was to make 100 non-engine-stop ascents. Hitherto no other vehicle, car or motorcycle, had succeeded in making more than 50 climbs in one day.

The Norton's first day logged 60 climbs and descents. There was one extremely brief engine stop when, during a replenishment pause, Pike accidentally knocked the throttle lever shut. He re-started so rapidly that Bourne did not even have time to look at his watch.

On the second day the remaining 40 climbs were reeled off and then the crew made for Edinburgh where it was turnabout for Birmingham, Plymouth, Land's End and back to Plymouth, the 'End' bit being added to bring the total mileage to the planned 1,500 (actually it was 1,531).

On the first day on 'the Bwlch' the engine ran continuously, except for the inadvertent stoppage, for 9 hours 15 minutes. Non-stop running time for the 40 ascents on the following day was 7 hours 22 minutes. During the nine days that the test lasted the only maintenance required was adjustment of chains, brakes and clutch, and lubrication of chains and gearbox. Repairs consisted of wiring up a rear chainguard that had shed its securing bolt.

Four 'Maudes' in a row . . . but that did not satisfy Nortons. For 1927 they thought up yet another stunt to demonstrate what they called their 'standard reliability'. This time an ACU engineer picked six 490 cc ohv engines from factory stock. These were fitted into frames at Brooklands and each machine was first driven over one lap of the outer circuit and then, without any further running-in, timed over the flying kilometre. All six registered speeds in the 80 to 83 mph bracket.

Two of the engines were then chosen by lots. One was taken over by Nigel Spring's équipe for an attack on the Double 12-hour record and the other was passed to Phil Pike to power his sidecar outfit for a long-distance ACU-observed road test.

The Brooklands attempt began at 8 am on Tuesday, October 18. With an engine that had not yet done more than five miles, the speed was at first held well in check below 60 mph. Then, in two-hour shifts, Nigel Spring, Chris Staniland and Jack Emerson kept it steady at 64 to 66 mph. At dusk Bert Denly took over. He was followed round the track by a 2-litre Lagonda car whose headlights showed the way—picking out rabbits that added to the hazards. Lapping regularly at around 64 mph, Denly took the machine up to 762¾ miles at 8 pm, the average for the first 12 hours being 63.57 mph.

After a night in a lock-up shed the Norton had its tappets adjusted before the attack continued. With stops for rider changes, fuel and oil and a rear tyre swop the machine was belted round the track all day. At 7.15 pm the old 500, 750 and 1,000 cc class records were broken and, when the second 12 hours run ended at 8 pm, the total distance covered was 1,494 miles 1,216 yards at an average speed of 62.28 mph.

Phil Pike's job was another of those Land's End to John o' Groats marathons. This time he was involved in an accident with a bus that crumpled the sidecar and bent the front forks. After straightening things out Pike, who 27 years later was killed in a south-coast air raid, carried on to complete 2,238 miles. But the test had not been done strictly to schedule and when the ACU competitions committee met to decide who should have the Maudes Trophy it went to the Ariel company for a 5,000-mile non-engine-stop journey.

In subsequent years the Trophy passed into the hands of many famous firms in recognition of amazing feats of endurance and speed, but after 1927 Norton did not try again.

Chapter 9

The camshaft engine

JUST AS THEY had been one of the last firms to rely on side valve engines for racing, Norton were in no great hurry to change from push-rods to an overhead camshaft. However, early in 1927 it was known that Walter Moore had an ohc unit in readiness for the TT and that it would be mounted in what was described as 'a new dual frame'. Details of these innovations were announced in May.

The new engine had the crankcase, flywheel, conrod, piston and cylinder barrel layout practically identical with that of the ohv machines, using the long-established 79 mm by 100 mm, 490 cc formula. An enclosed vertical shaft on the offside carried the drive from mainshaft to camshaft, with the 2:1 reduction shared between the two pairs of bevels so that the vertical shaft ran at considerably less than engine speed.

Two cams on a single shaft operated two-piece rockers which had hardened steel pads as cam followers and screw-and-locknut adjusters at the valve stem ends. The exhaust port, no longer in the fore-and-aft line, was offset slightly to allow the sweeping nearside pipe to clear the front down tube. A capacious tank on the seat pillar supplied oil to the dry sump double plunger pump built into the lower bevel box, and the magneto was mounted on a platform behind the cylinder, being chain-driven from a sprocket on the engine-shaft.

The engine was attached to a full cradle frame at no fewer than five points; the bases of the front down tube and the seat pillar were joined by a steel forging and the single top tube mated with a massively webbed steering head. Saddle stays and chain stays were reinforced by a pair of intermediate torque tubes to give great lateral rigidity and to provide an anchorage for the pivot-adjusted three-speed gearbox of new type that had the long, foot-operated gear lever attached directly to it. Hitherto gear levers, where not of the tank-side pattern, had been mounted on the seat pillar. It should be remembered that the positive-stop shift was still to come and selection of ratios by means of the lengthy Norton lever called for skilful and precise footwork.

Webb-type front forks, with friction disc shock absorbers and steering damper, 8 inch diameter

brakes and a handsome saddle tank—Nortons' first—made up the general specification.

For TT practising the factory sent to the Island a wagon-load of machines consisting of camshaft models, new, slightly modified push-rod units in the cradle frame and a miscellany of the previous year's engines in both open and cradle frames.

Alec Bennett, Joe Craig and Stanley Woods were all entered on, and practised with, camshaft mounts; Jimmy Shaw had one of the modified ohv models and Yorkshire's Ernie Searle and Australia's Len Stewart used 1926-engined jobs.

Very early in the training period Woods demonstrated the potential of the 'cammy' Norton, clocking a lap at 68.4 mph. Bennett's best was

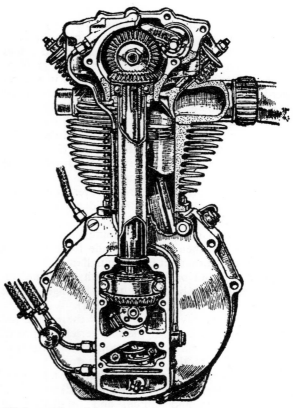

Walter Moore's overhead camshaft Norton engine (79 mm × 100 mm, 490 cc). At its first TT appearance in 1927 it provided Alec Bennett with a Senior race victory.

67.4 and Searle rode his ohv at 66.3. When practising ended Craig topped the Senior 'leader board' with a lap at 68.9 mph.

The practice session of 1927 was the last to be held over 'open' roads; for race days the course had always been closed to the public by virtue of a special Act of Tynwald, the Manx Parliament. But no such precaution had been taken for the early morning practices, which by 1927 had extended to cover nearly a fortnight. As speeds mounted into the 70 mph area many people became worried about the inherent danger but the authorities took no action. Then, on the eighth practice day of 1927, came the dreaded tragedy. C. A. C. (Archie) Birkin, brother of car racer 'Tim' Birkin and managing director of McEvoy Motorcycles, was swinging his Norton through the bend beyond Kirkmichael that still perpetuates his memory, when he collided, fatally, with a tradesman's van travelling the other way. During the remainder of that year's training, volunteers marshalled various points on the course and in 1928 the Tynwald Act included the full road closure measures that have applied ever since.

It was with 'quiet confidence' that the Bracebridge Street boys went to the Senior starting line. The camshaft machines had come through the preliminaries with flying colours. The factory team, Bennett, Craig and Woods, had shown encouraging speeds; they praised the handling qualities of the new frame and there had been hardly any new-model 'bugs'. Their main cause for anxiety appeared to come from the Sunbeam camp, now led by Graham Walker, with additional threats from Freddie Dixon on an HRD and Jimmy Simpson (AJS).

Nortons' hopes for a Manufacturers' Team Prize took a setback right at the start when Joe Craig's engine refused to fire and minutes were lost while he changed a sparking plug. Whether Alec Bennett was in difficulty or simply playing his calculated waiting game could not be determined, but he completed the first lap no higher than fifth. There was, however, no doubt about Stanley Woods's intentions; from a standing start he raised the lap record to 70.70 mph, and on his second circuit he put up another record—31 minutes 54 seconds, an average speed of 70.90—which was the first time 32 minutes had been beaten. Behind him came Dixon and Simpson. On the third lap Bennett was in third place and he moved into second on lap four.

Pit signalling in those days was a pretty hit-and-miss business and when Woods came in to re-fuel at the end of his fourth lap he was simply told that he was in the lead and had better press on. Had he known that he held a lead of some four minutes over Bennett it is unlikely that he would have maintained his ever-increasing gait. As it was he overworked his clutch climbing the Mountain and had to tour in to retire on the fifth lap. It was this experience that led the great Irish rider to develop his own private signalling system which, when used for the first time five years later, gained him one of the most spectacular victories in TT history.

So, with Woods out, Bennett headed the leader board with a comfortable margin over Tommy Spann (Sunbeam) and Tom Simister who, after so many years in Norton saddles, had switched to Triumph. Jimmy Shaw held his Norton in fourth berth, a position in which he finished.

The last lap saw a wild upheaval among the men chasing Bennett, who, incidentally, had finished his fifth tour with a fuel stop. Joe Craig, who had recouped his delayed start by working up to sixth place, retired and Ernie Searle, just off the leader board, broke a valve spring and pushed home to miss his replica by a few seconds.

Second place looked like a toss-up between Spann and Simister but when Spann went out it was seen that an entirely unconsidered dark horse was likely to spring a surprise.

From well down among the lower ranks of the field a virtual newcomer to the TT course, a young Scotsman by the name of J. Guthrie, had manoeuvred his New Hudson up to level peg with the veteran Simister. This Jimmy Guthrie, from the Lowlands textile town of Hawick, had made a mark at Brooklands and in speed trials, but his sole Island experience had been the previous Monday's Junior Race and a ride on a Matchless back in 1923—both outings resulting in retirements. He had not even ridden in the 'Amateur'. Yet here he was, on a marque that since 1911 had never had a better Senior placing than 14th, coming home to pip Simister by one second short of a full minute.

Bill Mansell, who in 1927 became Norton's managing director following the death of R. T. Shelley, took full note of this performance and it will be no surprise if I recall that Jim Guthrie's mounts for the 1928 TT races were Nortons.

So, even if Bracebridge Street had failed to gain the team prize (it went to the Sunbeam trio, Graham Walker, Charlie Dodson and Walter Birch) camshaft machines had brought home a Trophy won at record speed and had set up a record lap. Alec Bennett's eventual time advantage over the second man was 8 minutes 22 seconds and his speed over the seven laps averaged 68.41 mph.

To be fair it should be remembered that Stanley Woods's lead on the second place man on laps 1, 2, and 3 was respectively 53, 137 and 190 seconds and, despite a fuel stop after the fourth lap, he had that 4½-minute lead on Bennett when his clutch failed.

After the TT, Stanley, who since the previous year's race had been a full-time employee of Norton Motors, went on, with the 'cammy' model, to victories in the Dutch TT (that year elevated to International status) and the Grands Prix of Belgium and Switzerland. He was leading the French GP when he took a toss and Joe Craig carried the Norton banner to win by almost five minutes. At the Ulster GP Shaw won the 500 cc race at a record 74.18 mph—fastest speed for any road race yet held—and another Irishman, A. de Gourley was first in the unlimited category with a 588 cc push-rod machine.

It was in 1927 that Bert Denly's 490 cc push-rod Norton became the first 500 cc machine to beat 100 miles in the hour and a future Norton teamster, Percy (Tim) Hunt, began his road racing career with a record speed, record lap victory in the 'Amateur'.

The new-season's (1928) Norton range displayed at the 1927 Show was headed by production versions of the TT cradle frame machines. The ohc model, catalogued as the CS1 (camshaft one) had the external appearance of the cam gear tidied up, particularly around the lower bevel box, and the rectangular oil tank was replaced by a round-fronted container. The push-rod type was named the ES2, though nobody, so far as I can ascertain, now knows what the initial letters signified. Some maintain that they were intended to denote the Ernie Searle model since he had pioneered it in the

TT. Others say it referred to 'enclosed springs' because, for the first time, the return springs at the lower ends of the push-rods were encased in neat steel thimbles.

The whole range of machines had their silencers on the nearside, even the side valve Big Four and 16H achieved this by having their exhaust pipes curved round the front of the crankcase.

No fewer than 13 different motorcycles and four sidecar types constituted the full range and as an exercise in comparison with the present day it is worth listing the solos, all single-cylinder machines, and their prices. Lighting equipment was extra.

Cradle frame

CS1 - 490 ohc	£89	
ES2 - 490 ohv	£79	

Open frame

19 - 588 ohv	£66	
16H - 490 sv	£56	
2 - as 16H with touring equipment ...	£57	
24 - as 19 with 4-speeds	£71	
44 - as 24 with 'Colonial' frame	£72	10s
18 - 490 ohv	£63	10s
21 - as 18 with dry sump	£67	
34 - as 18 with 4-speeds	£68	10s
1 - 633 sv 'Big Four'	£60	5s
14 - as 1 with 4-speeds	£65	10s
17c - as 1 with 490 sv engine	£59	5s

As indicated in the previous chapter, for the first time in five years there was no Maudes Trophy on the Show stand, but the 'Honoratus board' of competition successes included the names of two Norton riders who were soon to become famous in reliability trials—G. B. Goodman and D. K. Mansell. (See Chapter 22.)

Chapter 10

350 cc Juniors

TALK OF A 'JUNIOR' Norton began to circulate early in 1928 and a few weeks before the TT the company announced that a 348 cc (71 mm × 88 mm) version of the push-rod ES2 would in fact be raced. When it appeared for practising it was seen to be, except for a 'shorter' cylinder barrel, virtually a replica of its bigger brother.

Two-race factory entries were made for the old brigade, Shaw, Craig and Woods. Bennett, being Velocette-mounted for the Junior, was booked for the Senior only, as was the newly engaged Tim Hunt, using his own machine. The other Norton new boy, Guthrie, was listed for both races. H. Matthews was provided with a 350 cc works engine and so became the first of a long line of privateers able to benefit from the easy interchangeability of the Norton power units. Ted Mellors and H. E. Hobbs, using their own machines, made up the silver-tank strength.

The 350 push-rod models were disappointing in practice and it was not until the sixth day that the Norton name appeared on the Junior leader board, when Joe Craig topped the table with a 348 *camshaft* version of the 490 ohc machine.

In the Senior category, Guthrie quickly showed form when, on the first morning, he made the second best performance to Sunbeam's Charlie Dodson, but Hunt injured himself in a fall at the 33rd Milestone on the third day and had to withdraw from the meeting.

On Junior race day not one Norton finished. The best showing was made by Jimmy Shaw who managed four laps before a broken valve spring put him out; Guthrie's machine caught fire at the pits; Matthews's broke a valve stem; Craig's bent a rocker arm and Woods's suffered slipped ignition timing.

Nor was the outcome much better in the Senior. After lying second for the first two laps, Joe Craig had just managed to get ahead when he fell and retired—both from the race and from motorcycle racing. For a time Woods occupied fourth place but he ultimately finished fifth and the only other Norton finisher was private owner Ted Mellors in sixth position. Falls and 'magneto trouble' (then the euphemism used to cover up almost every kind of breakdown) had eliminated the other seven starters.

After what can really only be described as a TT debacle, Nortons set off for the Continent, where Stanley Woods first won the Junior class of the Dutch TT with the 348 ohc model, and a week later, on the 490 type, took the French Grand Prix at Bordeaux with a record lap.

At the Nürburgring in July, Junior Nortons ridden by Italy's Pietro Ghersi and Scotland's Jimmy Guthrie were first and second in the 350 cc class of the German GP in which only six of the 18 starters finished, the third man being six minutes behind Guthrie.

Over in Erin's Isle Jimmy Shaw finished first on handicap in the 350 cc Ulster Grand Prix and became the Irish Champion.

Then in September Tim Hunt, recovered from his TT spill, won the Amateur TT for the second successive year—with a last lap at 71.05 mph, a record for the Island course in both amateur and professional classes. The previous best had been set by Stanley Woods at 70.90 mph in the 1927 Senior TT.

How Tim managed to squeeze a professional TT entry between two Amateur victories is explained in Chapter 18—which looks at the September series of Island races.

At the end of 1928 Nortons published a 'Chart of Annual Placings' in Isle of Man races over the years, back to 1920. It read as follows:

CHART OF ANNUAL PLACINGS

1920	Senior	2, 4, 7, 8, 10, 11, 13, 14
1921	„	6, 11, 12
1922	„	5, 10, 15, 21, 22
1923	„	2, 4, 5, 7, 14
„	Sidecar	2, 3
„	Amateur	6, 9, 11
1924	Senior	1, 5, 9, 10, 12
„	Sidecar	1, 5
„	Amateur	4, 8, 11
1925	Senior	3, 11, 13, 15, 16, 17
„	Sidecar	2, 3
„	Amateur	1, 2, 3, 7, 12, 13, 14, 16, 17
1926	Senior	1, 4, 11
„	Amateur	4, 20
1927	Senior	1, 4, 17
„	Amateur	1, 4, 5, 24
1928	Senior	5, 6
„	Amateur	1, 4, 5, 6, 7

Although not so impressive a record as was to follow in the 1930s, it was nevertheless a creditable reckoning of perseverance with growing success as the score of seven trophies in five years shows In only one race from 1920 did the company fail to see a Norton in the first six; this was in the first attempt at the Junior in 1928 when none of the five starters finished the course. In the period covered by the 'Chart' 170 Norton motorcycles had started in 19 races; 72 had finished the course and 98 had been marked 'retired'. However you work out the reliability ratio, there can be little doubt that racers of other makes must have felt that there were an awful lot of Nortons to be beaten!

Except for the fitting of saddle tanks and polished aluminium primary chain cases to all models, very little change was made to the range for 1929—but two 'surprises' were kept back for the Show. They were, predictably, 348 cc examples of the CS1 and the ES2. Apart from one obvious difference, they both looked almost exactly like their 490 cc counterparts. The 'difference' was that the rear frame omitted the extra torque tubes between seat and chain stays. Called Norton 'Juniors', the CJ camshaft machine was priced at £77 and the JE ohv cost £68.

For the 1929 racing season Walter Moore assembled a squad which, it seemed, could hardly fail to produce at least one winner. It lacked Bennett and Shaw but, to back up Woods and Guthrie, Tim Hunt and Jim Simpson were on the strength. This formidable quartet was destined to bring many honours to Bracebridge Street — but not in 1929.

This really was a black year. One after another disasters beset the racing department so that when the season ended the compilers of the company's advertisements had very little to shout about. Of the TT the best they could find to say was that 'The Norton, as usual, was well in the picture'. Let's get the sad story over and done with quickly.

Woods, Hunt and Simpson all rode in both the Junior and Senior events, but Guthrie did the Junior only. All except Hunt, who was fourth in the Senior (after two falls which robbed him of both footrests), retired in both races. Douglas Lamb, the only non-works Junior contestant, crashed fatally in the Senior at Greeba Bridge. The accident was a 'pile-up' in which oil was spilled on the road and Simpson fell heavily on the slippery surface, suffering a leg injury that kept him out of racing for the rest of the season.

Abroad, Tim Hunt won the 500 cc class of the European Grand Prix. The sidecar class was won by Bill Mansell's son, Dennis, who at 19 was already an acknowledged expert on three wheels. He and Graham Goodman, who rode solos and sidecars equally well, had collected between them a load of awards in reliability trials. In this field Norton successes included the chief prizes in such important open trials as the Travers Trophy, the Bemrose Trophy, the Cotswold Cups, the Patland Cup, the Western Centre Trophy and the Welsh Trophy.

Late-season encouragement for the road racing department came with first and third placings in the Amateur TT.

So, as the 1920s gave way to the 1930s, Nortons rang up their score of major successes in the following terms:

Five times winner Tourist Trophy Races
Four times winner French Grand Prix
Four times winner Amateur TT
Four times winner Maudes Trophy
Five times winner Belgian GP
Seven times winner Ulster GP
Twice winner South African TT
Four times winner Brooklands 200 miles Sidecar Race
Four times winner Dutch TT
Winner 350 cc German GP 1928
Winner Brooklands Sidecar GP three times in succession
First 500 cc machine to cover 100 miles in one hour

19: (*Above*) *The team that won the 1926 International Six Days Trial Trophy for Great Britain line up after the speed test at Brooklands track. Left to right: Graham Walker (493 Sunbeam); Phil Pike and Dr G. H. S. Letchworth (588 Norton sc); and Jack Lidstone (495 James twin).*

20: (*Right*) *Stanley Woods passes the pits in the 1927 Senior TT aboard the new ohc Norton on which he raised the lap record to 70.90 mph. On a similar machine Alec Bennett won the race at 68.41 mph.*

21: *On a standard Model CSI which he had previously ridden in the Scottish Six Days Trial, Tim Hunt won the 1928 Amateur TT and achieved the unique feat of being the only rider ever to set the September lap record at a higher speed than the then-existing TT figure. The Manx MCC official in the blazer is the Rev Bertie Reid, later Geoff Duke's father-in-law.*

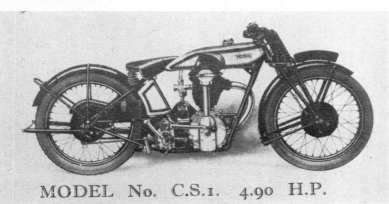

MODEL No. C.S.I. 4.90 H.P.

22: *Compare the engine of this 1929 Model CS1 with those in pictures 20 and 21; Woods's oil pump is a separate unit; on Hunt's machine it is in one piece with the timing chest; there is only one external oil pipe on this latest model.*

23: *In 1931 the Arthur Carroll-designed ohc engine began its history as the greatest of all single-cylinder racing units. Jimmy Guthrie, second to Tim Hunt in the Junior TT, shakes hands with his entrant, Nigel Spring.*

24: *First to lap the TT course at 60 and 70 mph, Jim Simpson broke the 80 mph barrier in the 1931 Senior, and is seen here working on it at Ballig Bridge. Team mates Hunt, Guthrie and Woods made it the first of Nortons' string of 12 TT 'trebles'.*

25: *One of the great all-rounders of the inter-wars period, Jack Williams, the 'Cheltenham Flyer', and his 1933 Senior mount.*

26: *Astride their 1934 Senior TT mounts are, left to right: Jimmy Guthrie, the winner; Jimmy Simpson, runner-up; and Vic Brittain, another outstanding racing trialsman, who was fifth. They won the Manufacturers' Team Prize outright. Standing are mechanic Bill Mewis, Arthur Carroll, Joe Craig, Gilbert Smith, Bill Mansell, mechanic Frank Sharratt and Dennis Mansell.*

27: (*Above*) *Londoner Harold Daniell gained his first Island win in the 1933 Senior Manx GP. Following him here is the runner-up, also Norton mounted, Dr J. K. Swanston.*

28: (*Left*) *Winner of the 1933 Senior Manx GP, Harold Daniell, aboard the International model that had also carried him to second place in 1932. With him is J. K. Swanston, who broke the lap record. Nortons filled the first five places.*

29: (*Above*) *One of the greats of motorcycle racing, Walter Hand-ley rode only one season on Norton works models—in 1934. Here, in that year's Ulster GP, he is shooting Balloo Bridge on the all-out, seven-mile Clady Straight in his last road race.*

30: (*Right*) *Jimmy Guthrie, winner of the Junior TT for the second year running in 1935 seen with three of Nortons' race department* maestri, *development engineer Joe Craig, designer Arthur Carroll and super mechanician Bill Mewis.*

31: *Prepared by Joe Craig to run on alcohol fuel and ridden by Guthrie, this 500 cc Norton lifted the World's One Hour record to 114.092 mph on the Montlhéry track, near Paris, in 1935. In one day, 15 world's records were broken—in addition to the Hour, the 50 kilos, 50 miles, 100 kilos and 100 miles, in 500, 750 and 1,000 cc classes.*

32: *Front wheel airborne, rear tyre part flattened, the Norton hits a Montlhéry bump during Jim Guthrie's 1935 attack on the Hour record.*

33: *This Norton, specially built for Bob Holliday in 1936, was never catalogued. The long push-rods indicate a Model 19 596 cc engine; frame is an ES2 type.*

34: *In 1935 Stanley Woods (Guzzi) beat Jim Guthrie (Norton) to win the Senior TT by 4 secs. In 1936, when this picture was taken, Jim had reversed the order, beating the Irishman, then Velocette-mounted, by 18 secs. Stanley was the fastest lapper in both years.*

35: *Ken Bills offers Freddie Frith a toffee as they meet, after wartime separation, on the Douglas quayside.*

36: *Freddie Frith, first to put the TT lap speed above 90 mph in 1937, with his wife, Julia, and Nigel Spring at the Donington circuit in 1939.*

37: *Harold Daniell hurls his 1938 Senior Norton down Bray Hill on his way to his first TT victory and the first-ever under 25-minute, 91-mph, record lap that was destined to stand for 12 years.*

Chapter 11

Racing into the 1930s

THE 1930s were truly glamour years for Norton. All around the globe riders of Bracebridge Street bikes plucked the prize plums from practically every branch of international motorcycle sport. In the eight years from 1931 to 1938 Nortons won every Senior and Junior Isle of Man TT except the 1935 Senior and the 1938 Junior.

But this eventful decade began with a world-wide depression and ended with a world-wide war. The effects of the Wall Street stock market crash had crossed the Atlantic rapidly and 1930 saw Europe struggling with a slump. The British motor-cycle industry was as badly hit as any and many long-established marques disappeared altogether, forced out of business by economic conditions they could not surmount. Others, particularly the bigger factories, were compelled to retrench drastically, cut their prices and generally tighten their purse strings.

Nevertheless, somehow the sport carried on. Despite dole queues, hunger marches, means tests and soup kitchens, enthusiasm for motorcycling burned strongly. It is even possible that, in a roundabout way, the two-wheeler industry actually gained some benefit, for citizens needing mobility as they chased and changed jobs bought motor-cycles and bicycles instead of cars they could not afford. It was in this period that the sidecar trade expanded enormously and the cycling movement grew to such an extent that by the late 1930s there were reckoned to be 14 million pedallers using British roads.

In Bracebridge Street, while the sales staff and production people were coping with their special problems, things were also happening in the racing department. Walter Moore had left for Neckarsulm, Germany, to produce a camshaft machine for NSU. Joe Craig had succeeded him as development engineer and a young man named Arthur Carroll had re-designed the Norton racing engine. Carroll, whose untimely death in a road accident in 1935 robbed motorcycling of one of its best technicians, had joined the company, after serving an engineering apprenticeship, in James Norton's time. He was imbued with the founder's belief that the best way to make things work well was to make them simple, both to build and to maintain.

Retaining the basics of the original ohc engine, Carroll radically altered the camshaft and magneto drive layout. He discarded Moore's smoothly sur-faced timing chest and replaced it with the 'square-sided' bevel box and offside magneto chain arrangement that was from then on to distinguish ohc Nortons. At the same time he created 'built-in' ease of maintenance. Private owners and mechanics throughout the world, working against the clock to replace a piston, change a compression ratio or extract a bent valve, have been thankful for the easy way in which Norton units could be pulled apart and re-assembled.

So it came about that, just as the firm settled on a type of single-cylinder racing engine that was to continue for many years, the Auto-Cycle Union stabilised the TT races into a pattern that remained undisturbed up to the advent of the Second World War.

Previously, right from the first race in 1907, there had been constant changes in the set-up. The original 'Short Course' had been replaced by the Mountain Circuit, which itself had been altered and lengthened. There had been many variations in the rules, and experiments with different capa-city classes and additional races like the Sidecar and Ultra-Lightweight events.

The formula, established by the time the 1930s opened, was a simple and straightforward one. The programme consisted of three solo races, held in a week early in June. On Monday there was the Junior race (under 350 cc); Wednesday was devoted to the Lightweight (under 250 cc) class; and Friday rounded the meeting off with the Senior (under 500 cc) event. All three races were run over seven laps of the 37.73-mile Mountain Course, a total distance of 264¼ miles.

Actually, the first lap was a slightly short one because, for spectator interest, the starting point was sited opposite the central seating section of the Grandstand, while the real 'start-and-finish' line was by the timekeepers' hut, some 20 or so yards back up the course.

The Mountain Course of the 1930s covered exactly the same route as it does today. Over the years it has been subjected to re-surfacing, widen-ing and broadening of corners, just as any road normally used for public traffic is bound to be, but the centre-line distance has barely changed at all.

A 37¾-mile lap begins and ends on the Glen-crutchery Road, a stretch of residential thorough-fare high up behind the Island's capital town Douglas. In an area of parkland are located all the usual appurtenances of a motor race—grandstand replenishment pits, scoreboards, paddock, offices, first-aid quarters, refreshment facilities and so forth.

The scoring system is unusual because of the way in which 'interval start' TT races are run. With an interval start, as opposed to a massed start, riders are dispatched one at a time, or in pairs or small batches. In this way they ride 'against the clock' and it does not necessarily follow that the first man to complete the full course distance is the winner. It may—and often does—happen that a rider who was a late starter ends up with the shortest overall time. This method may not be as easy for the spectator to follow as a massed start, but for many folk it adds interest and excitement.

For the crowds at the start there are duplicated main scoreboards facing the full length of the Grandstand. On each board, below each rider's number is a progress dial marked with letters re-ferring to various points on the course. A rider's arrival at each point is shown by a moving finger. Above these 'clocks', as they are called, are coloured lamps which flash to warn the pit attendants of the imminent approach of the sig-nalled riders.

Coloured number cards below the clocks show which lap each rider is on. NS stands for 'non starter', R for 'retired' and F signifies a finisher. Below the cards are sections on which are painted the growing times, lap by lap. Additional score-boards show the six lap leaders, their lap times, speeds and course speeds.

Thus Grandstand spectators are given virtually a complete picture of what is going on all through the race. Onlookers around the course have to work it out for themselves or rely on the several public address stations which broadcast news re-layed from the Grandstand as the race commentator makes his announcements. An experienced, dedi-cated TT fan, armed with scorecard and stop-watch, gets almost as much fun out of keeping his own time checks on his favourite riders as he does from watching them in action.

Many writers have tried to 'explain' the TT course. In fact, it defies description. Even when you have seen it and assimilated its intricacies it is still almost impossible to believe that its 37¾ miles, 200-plus corners, mountain sweeps, dog-legs and hairpins were covered in Diamond Jubilee year (1967) in nearly 20 minutes at almost 109 mph.

Maps can do little more than pinpoint place names. The best I can do for those who have never seen this fantastic circuit is to add a touch of 'contour' and general background. No sooner has the rider swept past the Grandstand than he is faced with the awesome plunge down Bray Hill. From the bottom-gear corner at Quarter Bridge, there are some seven miles of undulating, writhing road through villages and hamlets to another sharp right-hander at Ballacraine. Turning northward the road runs level through a valley past Laurel Bank and at Glen Helen climbs a short, sharp hill to emerge on to a lengthy, fast stretch punctuated by 'easy there!' hazards such as those at the 11th Milestone and Handley's Cottage. Grim determina-tion is needed to blast full bore down Baaregarroo Hill and through the blind bend at its foot; the curves that follow into Kirkmichael village call for the highest degree of concentration. Five miles of high-speed swinging, with a leap at Ballaugh Bridge, lead to the Sulby Straight and the right-left turns by the Ginger Hall Hotel that preface the eastwards ride into the centre of Ramsey town.

Now comes the six-mile ascent of the Snaefell Mountain. Ramsey Hairpin, Waterworks Corner, Gooseneck and The Cutting are taken in quick succession and precede the hillside climb along the Mountain Mile and thence to the deceptive bends that turn into the Verandah—a curving stretch the outside edge of which seems to drop away sheer into the port of Laxey miles below.

The Snaefell Mountain Railway tracks are crossed at The Bungalow (once a hotel, now a tram shelter) and a few hundred yards farther on the highest point is reached—1,350 feet up.

It is practically all downhill now, but there is still a lot to contend with—the three lefts before Windy Corner, the Corner itself, the 33rd Mile-stone complex, Keppel Gate and the dive from Kate's Cottage to the right-angle at Creg-ny-Baa. Then there is the furious swoop through Brandish Corner to Hillberry . . . up the little hill at Cronk-ny-Mona . . . sharp right at Signpost Corner . . . left at Bedstead . . . round the hairpin at Governor's Bridge . . . into the Dip and out on to the Glencrutchery Road with the bunting on the Grandstand beckoning in the distance. And that's just one lap!

The rules governing the races in the 1930s per-mitted supercharging and streamlining but special 'dope' fuels were barred; the only variation allowed from straight petrol was a mixture of petrol and benzole—and not more than 50% of the latter.

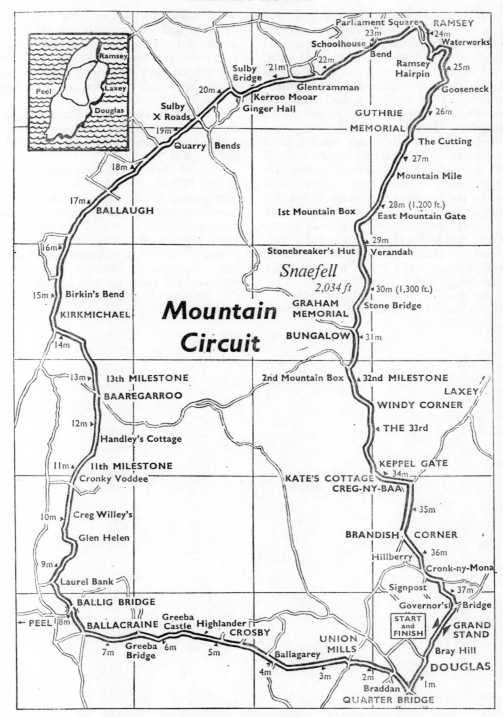

Parliament Square
23m
RAMSEY
24m
Waterworks
Schoolhouse
22m
Bend
Ramsey
Hairpin
25m
Sulby
21m
Bridge
Glentramman
Gooseneck
20m
Kerroo Mooar
Ginger Hall
GUTHRIE
MEMORIAL
26m
Sulby
X Roads
19m
The Cutting
27m
Quarry Bends
Mountain Mile
18m
28m (1,200 ft.)
17m
BALLAUGH
1st Mountain Box
East Mountain Gate
29m
16m
Stonebreaker's Hut
Verandah

Snaefell
2,034 ft
30m (1,300 ft.)

15m
Birkin's Bend
KIRKMICHAEL
GRAHAM
MEMORIAL
Stone Bridge

Mountain
Circuit
BUNGALOW
31m

14m
13m
13th MILESTONE
BAAREGARROO
2nd Mountain Box
32nd MILESTONE
LAXEY
WINDY CORNER
12m
Handley's Cottage
THE 33rd

11m
11th MILESTONE
Cronky Voddee
KEPPEL GATE
34m
KATE'S COTTAGE
CREG-NY-BAA
10m
Creg Willey's
Glen Helen
35m
BRANDISH CORNER
9m
Laurel Bank
Hillberry
36m
Cronk-ny-Mona
BALLIG BRIDGE
Signpost
37m
PEEL
8m
BALLACRAINE
Greeba
Castle Highlander
CROSBY
Governor's
Bridge
START
and
FINISH
GRAND
STAND
7m
Greeba
Bridge
6m
5m
Ballagarey
UNION
MILLS
Bray Hill
DOUGLAS
4m
3m
2m
Braddan
1m
QUARTER BRIDGE

The Isle of Man TT Mountain Course, 37¾ miles of continuously twisting road, varying
from sea level to over 1,300 feet. Adopted in 1911, it has been used virtually as shown
ever since, and is the world's toughest testing ground for motorcycle development.
Shell-Mex-BP.

Anyone who was a member of a motorcycle club affiliated to the FICM (Fédération Internationale des Clubs Motocyclistes, the world governing body of motorcycling sport, later the FIM) could enter, but to race it was necessary to achieve certain 'qualifying' standards during the practising periods.

During a race a rider could stop to make adjustments and repairs, but only with the equipment he carried with him. Outside assistance of any kind was taboo. Even the kindly meant helping hand from a bystander when restarting could—and did—and still does—bring disqualification. Any repairs or replacements that needed parts or tools not carried by the rider had to be dealt with at his Grandstand depot where just his pit attendant could help, only using equipment already in the pit. Even replacement parts had to be of the same brand or make as that specified prior to the race. For example, a man could not start with one make of sparking plug and change in mid-race to another.

On the day before each race, machines were 'weighed-in' — a term deriving from horse-racing parlance and not actually involving the use of scales. Scrutineers examined the machines for safety and conformity with the rules, after which the mounts were locked up and not touched by anyone until their riders had access to them shortly before the start of the race.

After each race the official measurers and chemists checked the successful machines to ensure that engine capacities were not exceeded and that the fuel was 'legal'.

Most of these regulations and customs, which by the 1930s had evolved from previous experience, remain in force today, with the main exception of supercharging which was prohibited in the post-Second World War period. In the main they applied also to the Amateur TT (later the Manx Grand Prix) which followed in September each year, and the mechanical requirements were generally the same for the International Grands Prix, though these were invariably massed-start events.

Chapter 12

Hat-tricks and doubles

FOR THE 1930 racing season Joe Craig's team consisted of Stanley Woods, Jim Simpson and Tim Hunt. Jimmy Guthrie had transferred to AJS. Even before Arthur Carroll's new engines were tried in the Isle of Man, Nortons had some reason to hope for success for, in a pre-TT gallop, Hunt had won the 350 cc class of Northern Ireland's North West 200 race. This was one of several Irish road races which were held early in the year and which the English manufacturers used as try-outs for their new season's wares.

Though possessing no motorcycle factories of its own, Erin's Isle has provided a long line of magnificent racing men right from the start of the game. For a number of years the Ulster Grand Prix was the world's fastest motorcycle road race, and some of the very earliest speed events in motoring history were held in Dublin's Phoenix Park.

It was an Irishman, H. G. Tyrell Smith, who opened the 1930 TT series by leading the Rudge team to its famous 1-2-3 Junior victory. Nortons could do nothing against this onslaught from the Coventry factory, which also mounted Ernie Nott, Graham Walker and (in the Senior only) Walter Handley. The first Junior Norton home (in sixth place) was ridden by Woods; Hunt finished ninth and Simpson retired.

In the horribly wet Senior event, Simpson was the only survivor of the Norton team. By finishing third to Handley and Walker, he prevented another Rudge hat-trick and for the first time in eight years of TT racing he completed the course on a Senior machine. This achievement caused Bracebridge Street publicists to advertise that 'the Norton company provided a machine Simpson couldn't break'!

In the Ulster Grand Prix, Jimmy Simpson became the world's fastest road racer with a record lap at 84.63 mph before he blew his machine up, leaving Woods to win the race at an average of 80.56 mph. A month later Stanley Woods won the 500 cc class in the French Grand Prix, his Norton being the only machine to finish!

Even though the TT results had not come up to expectations, a post-season assessment of the new engines must have convinced Nortons that there was not much wrong with them and if Craig and Carroll found any bugs that needed sorting-out they kept quiet, for the 1931 TT models showed very little alteration. The disposition of the inlet port was slightly revised and the four-speed Sturmey-Archer gearboxes were fitted with positive-stop control. Woods, Simpson and Hunt were again factory entries and Guthrie was back on silver tank machines entered by Nigel Spring.

The Junior race was dramatic throughout, with the stars rising and waning on the scoreboard as a terrific battle between Birmingham's Nortons, Coventry's Rudges and Wolverhampton's 'Ajays' was fought out. With one lap gone Simpson and Woods were first and second, ahead of Freddie Hicks (AJS) and Ernie Nott (Rudge). Guthrie lay fifth and Tim Hunt, delayed by having to replace a detached plug terminal was eighth.

By lap four Hicks had retired. Hunt had whirled up to second spot behind Simpson, replacing Woods who, struggling with a broken steering damper, had dropped to fifth. Guthrie had taken third place at Nott's expense.

'Unlucky Jim' found himself in trouble while climbing the Mountain on lap six. His engine was misfiring and he coasted past Windy Corner convinced that something irreparable had happened. Halting at the 33rd Milestone for an inspection, he found nothing more seriously wrong than a blocked jet, but the stoppage dropped him from the lead to 12th place.

The order of the leaders on the last lap did not change; Hunt stayed just ahead of Guthrie, and Woods was unable to pass Nott. Simpson moved up to finish eighth. All four of the stars finished; and the works team won both the Manufacturers' and the Club team prizes. During the course of the race the previous year's lap record was broken by Norton riders no fewer than 21 times. Tim Hunt's whirlwind fourth lap was the ultimate best at 75.27 mph, just five seconds outside 30 minutes. His race average was 73.94 mph.

Despite general belief that Nortons could not hope to better their Junior performance, Friday's race turned out to be an even more spectacular success, resulting in the Senior's first one-make hat-trick since the Indian treble in 1911. Norton riders occupied first, second and third places on every lap and broke the lap record 18 times. On the first circuit Guthrie led from a standing start at 77.61 mph. Simpson, Woods and Hunt followed—all at over 77 mph and all above the 1930 record lap speed. On lap two Simpson took the lead at 78.80 mph and the other three all lapped at over 78 mph.

Onlookers gasped when the third lap speeds were posted. Jimmy Simpson, first man to lap at 60 mph (1924 Junior) and at 70 mph (1926 Senior) had now beaten the 80 mark. At just one second outside 28 minutes, his speed was 80.82 mph, including a slow down to refill a nearly bone-dry tank! But once again Jim's luck was out and a crash at Ballaugh Bridge reduced his machine to scrap and cost Norton the makers' team prize, which was not awarded that year.

His stablemates, Hunt, Guthrie and Woods, kept Bracebridge Street in the first three places to the end of the race, pit signals telling them to ease off on the final circuit. So Tim Hunt, who had beaten the 1930 record on every lap except the last, became the first man to win the Senior and Junior races in the same week. His average lap time for the whole Senior race was 29 minutes 4 seconds—37 seconds better than the previous year's record lap. His average speed for the race was 77.90 mph.

The team went on to a triumphant tour of the Continental circuits and rounded-off the season with an 86.43 mph Ulster Grand Prix win for Woods and a 350 cc class win for Leo Davenport—who had paired with Guthrie as a Norton works rider in the Junior category.

At a pre-TT warm-up, the Leinster '200', in which Guthrie won the 350 and Woods the 500 cc classes, it was seen that the Norton engines for 1932 had gained some extra cylinder barrel finning but a greatly increased use of alloy metals indicated much lighter machines.

The Junior TT had all the marks of another Norton/Rudge duel, with Bracebridge Street's 'Big Four'—Woods, Simpson, Guthrie and Hunt —lined up against Wal Handley, Ernie Nott, Graham Walker and Tyrell Smith. At the finish Woods was the only survivor of the Norton quartet—in first place which he had held throughout the race, averaging 77.16 mph and raising the lap record by over 3 mph to 78.62 mph. All four Norton men bettered the 1931 lap record from a standing start on the opening lap. Hunt retired on the second lap with a broken rocker arm and the two Jims both ran out of road.

Friday's Senior was a royal occasion, for Prince George was among the spectators, and on the very first lap he saw Simpson open up with a 'four score' speed of 80.11 mph. Woods followed him closely; Guthrie, in fifth place, was behind Handley and Nott. Tim Hunt, not having a lucky year, was out of the race within the first two miles, having collided with Braddan Bridge. To add to his chagrin, he was one of the Norton team nominated for the Manufacturers' award.

Around half distance Simpson reported at his pit that he was having difficulty changing gear through a sticking clutch lever. He managed to hang on to second place behind Woods but on the last lap Guthrie, who had worked his way past Handley and Nott, overhauled him. Woods, Guthrie and Simpson all finished, in that order, in less than the previous year's winning time, and Simpson on the second circuit raised his own lap record to 81.50 mph.

In two successive Seniors Norton had pulled off the hat-trick.

Chapter 13

Two Jims, Tim and Stanley

PROBABLY AS A CONSEQUENCE of Jimmy Simpson's gear changing trouble, the 1933 TT Nortons had a redesigned, neater foot-change mechanism. Long pressed-steel clutch and brake levers replaced the former brass components, and a new type of steering damper was also fitted. The 500 cc weighed 312 lb and the 350 cc, 298 lb—disproving the belief that the Junior type was the heavier because the 'hole in the cylinder was smaller'.

The 1933 Junior TT was a sweeping success for the Norton foursome who made a race of it among themselves with all the others nowhere. Those words 'among themselves' need an explanation. At one time Norton works men were instructed to conform to a pre-conceived race plan and to obey pit signals devised as the race developed. In 1931 this 'ride-to-orders' system had gone wrong and Bill Mansell had ordained that henceforth, as far as the TT was concerned, there would be no 'after-you-Claude' practices. Whatever might be arranged on the Continent, on the Island it was to be every man for himself and this policy remained in force for many years.

So, in the 1933 Junior the 'Big Four', regardless of the opposition, went at it hammer and tongs. Woods got down to it straight away and led throughout with Simpson, Hunt and Guthrie in full pursuit in that order.

On the fifth lap Hunt broke the lap record, with a 78.85 mph circuit. Woods shrugged off this challenge with a sixth lap at 79.22 mph. Saving his supreme effort for the final lap, Simpson was well on his way to a first-time Junior '80' when Dame Fortune dealt him another of her backhanders and blew up his engine at his *bête noire*, Ballaugh. Meanwhile there was suspense at the Grandstand. Woods, riding No 16, finished with a race average of 78.08 mph and sat back to await the arrival of Hunt, No 30.

When the Lancashire lad swept over the finish line there were tense moments while the time-keepers checked their figures. Then came the announcement—the Irishman had won by seven seconds! Guthrie's third place gave Nortons their first Junior 1-2-3. Only Norton machines equalled the 1932 race or record lap speeds.

Now really feeling their form, the 'Big Four' went at it again in the Senior race, coming up with a 1-2-3-4 result that pulverised the opposition. Again Woods was unassailable, achieving his fourth TT victory in two successive years. His winning speed of 81.04 mph represented a 4 minutes 5 seconds improvement over his 1932 race time. Simpson, second man home, was handicapped from the fifth lap by loss of brake efficiency following a record fourth tour at 82.74 mph. Hunt, who had to change an oiled plug at the start, was third. Guthrie in fourth berth at 79.49 mph was the only one of the quartet who did not beat the 80 mph mark for a race average. With Hunt and Simpson he formed the team which took both the Manufacturers' and the Club Team awards.

And so the 'unapproachable' foursome went on to the customary International Grands Prix ride-about, already known as the Continental Circus. In those days there was no World Championship, the later arrangement whereby champion riders and champion manufacturers were decided annually by counting points gained in certain selected races. (It was not until after the Second World War that the World Championship was instituted.) In the 1930s the title Championship of Europe was bestowed on different International events year by year. In one year it could be the Dutch TT, the next the French GP, and so on.

In one country after another—Holland, France, Belgium, Switzerland and Spain—the pattern of Norton success was woven, with the 'Big Four' divided into pairs, a couple for the 350 class and another for the 500. All through the season it was Norton 1-2 in each class, except in the Dutch TT where Hunt dropped his second place in the Senior while duelling with Woods on the last lap.

For the Ulster Grand Prix in August the pattern changed a little. In the 350 cc class the Bracebridge Street entries were Guthrie and Simpson, who emerged first and second on handicap. For the Senior a full team was entered, consisting of Woods, Hunt and a 'new boy' from Ireland's seemingly inexhaustible fund of brilliant racing motorcyclists, Walter Rusk. This fair-haired Ulsterman, known as the 'Blond Bombshell', had made his first appearance on the TT circuit in the previous June, failing to finish on a Sunbeam; but he had a high reputation on his

TO17434

native heath and Joe Craig's wisdom in bringing him into the Norton team was to pay off. From the start he lay second to Woods right through the 'world's fastest motorcycle race', in which Stanley covered the first three laps at an average of 89.06 mph and finished at a record 87.16 mph. Though Tim Hunt, delayed by a minor spill, could not make it a 1-2-3, he finished fourth and the team prize went to Norton.

But it was the last time that Tim was to receive a chequered flag. A few weeks later came the Swedish GP, that year's Grand Prix d'Europe. Jimmy Simpson had scooped up the 350 cc race with Jimmy Guthrie close astern. Stanley and Tim were about to repeat the formula in the 500 cc bout when their 'line' through a very fast bend was blocked by a Norwegian rider who was coasting home and fiddling with his carburettor. Woods saw the danger in time to dodge it; Hunt was a fraction too late. A broken thigh took years to mend and the damaged leg was set $2\frac{1}{2}$ inches shorter than the other.

After his wonderful ride in the 'Ulster' it was generally expected that Walter Rusk would line up under the Norton banner for 1934. Instead, his talents were secured for services aboard Velocettes, and to replace Tim Hunt in the Bracebridge Street brigade came Walter Handley.

The main change in the new season's race models was the use of hairpin valve springs for the first time. The previous year's bronze alloy cylinder head was otherwise unchanged but there was deeper finning on the steel-linered light-alloy barrel and two additional fins were cast on to the top of the crankcase, which had larger stiffening ribs. An oil scraper ring was fitted on the piston, while a new tank mounting employed four rubber-bushed vertical bolts running through tubes formed in the tank shell.

Guthrie, Simpson and Handley were teamed for the Junior TT event and they made a terrific race of it. The Scot led throughout with Simpson chasing him furiously. There were never more than a few seconds between them—at the finish the gap was nine seconds, Guthrie's average being 79.16 mph. On the second circuit he bumped the Junior lap record over the 80 mark to 80.11 mph.

With six laps nearly completed it was looking like another Norton hat-trick when Walter Handley dropped his mount at Governor's Bridge and so damaged his nose that he was compelled to retire. As he was not fit enough to ride in the Senior, the Junior was Handley's last Island ride. He went on to take part in the Continental Circus

with the Norton boys, but at the end of the season he hung up his helmet, having in the course of 12 years of racing contested 28 TTs, winning four trophies.

So, when it came to Friday's Senior race, Jim Guthrie was the only *official* Norton starter. Simpson, having ceased to work for Bracebridge Street, was down in the programme as a private entrant, as was Vic Brittain. Nevertheless, they were all three nominated as the Norton trio for the Manufacturers' Team prize. Brittain, famous as a trials rider, had ridden modestly in the TT since 1930 and had finished ninth on a Velocette in the Monday's Junior. Another celebrated all-rounder, Jack Williams, was also Norton-mounted, as was Norman Gledhill, a previous winner from the Manx Grand Prix.

The race was run in shocking weather. Guthrie took the lead and held it all the way. Woods, on one of the new 'foreign menaces', a Swedish Husqvarna, chased him hard but fell victim to the 'Husky's' notorious thirst when he ran out of fuel on the last lap, having made the fastest lap at 80.49 mph. Simpson moved into second place and Walter Rusk's Velocette was third. An honourable fifth place for Vic Brittain secured for Norton both the Manufacturers' and Club team prizes, the former being won outright. As with Handley, it was Jimmy Simpson's last TT. In the Lightweight race on the Wednesday, riding a Rudge, he had achieved his one and only Island victory after 12 long years of fighting with a vindictive Lady Luck—and he went out in a blaze of glory. In addition to his Tourist Trophy he secured 350 cc wins in the Grands Prix of Holland, Belgium, Germany, Switzerland and Ulster. In the 500 cc class he took the Swiss GP.

In the 26 TT races he contested between 1922 and 1934 Jimmy Simpson only twice finished outside the first three—he was fifth in the 1923 Sidecar event and eighth in the 1931 Junior. His single victory was in his last year; he was second four times, and third on four occasions. In a dozen years he raced only four makes of motor-cycle—Scott (once, in his first year); Rudge (once, in his last year); AJS (12 times, 1923 to 1928); and Norton (12 times, 1929 to 1934).

The first rider to cover a TT race lap at 60 mph, 70 mph and 80 mph, he made eight fastest laps in his time, his best-ever being at 81.50 mph in the 1932 Senior on a Norton.

In 1948 the Jimmy Simpson Trophy was donated as a special award for the fastest TT lappers.

Chapter 14

The Guthrie-Woods duels

AS THEY ENTERED the second half of the 1930s Nortons needed to re-stock their racing team, and to back up their Scottish ace Jimmy Guthrie they recaptured Irishman Walter Rusk and enlisted Englishman J. H. White. The last-named, by this time a schoolmaster, was already known as 'Crasher' White, having 'earned' the sobriquet after some spectacular upsets while racing with the Cambridge University club. In four successive Manx Grand Prix seasons he had twice finished well up on a Velocette and had won the 1934 Junior event on a Norton. He had, therefore, no TT experience when he found himself one of the 1935 Bracebridge Street works entries. He was not a Senior entry, however, and was not nominated for the official team. The third man with Guthrie and Rusk was Johnny Duncan, using Nortons for the first time after having ridden Raleighs, Cottons and New Imperials since 1928.

Mechanical changes for the new season included a new type of more tightly coiled hairpin valve springs and complete enclosure for the rocker gear. Other alterations included a four-gallon tank and a Norton-made four-speed gearbox which had integral foot-change mechanism, while aluminium finning was added to the brake drums.

Though Monday's weather was dry for the Junior event there was a strong wind blowing across the Mountain which prevented record speeds. Guthrie, Rusk and White were in line astern from the start and finished that way. On the third circuit, but for a refuelling stop, Rusk would have broken the lap record, his time of 28 minutes 19 seconds being only 3 seconds outside it. He and White engaged in a furious duel, the schoolmaster heading the Ulsterman on the first, second and fourth laps. By winning at 79.14 mph Guthrie recorded his second successive Junior win and Nortons' fifth.

By finishing seventh Duncan contributed to yet another Manufacturers' Team prize. Neither the 1933 nor the 1934 winning speeds were bettered by any machine other than a Norton and the company had gained its fifth TT hat-trick in five years.

The 1935 Senior was one of the most sensational races in the TT's long history. And thousands of spectators had to go home without seeing it because impossible weather conditions compelled the stewards to postpone it until the following day.

The Norton camp sent its men to the start line feeling pretty confident. Their chief threat, Stanley Woods, who was riding a Guzzi 120 degree angle twin, had not noticeably upset the balance of power during practising—but you never knew with Stanley, and Guthrie and Co had firm orders not to hang about. None of them, particularly Guthrie, needed any prodding and the Scot immediately took the lead with a first lap of 84.23 mph that smashed all existing records. Rusk was close behind and Woods lay third. On lap two Guthrie raised his speed to 84.81 mph.

But Woods, after a deceptively 'slow' start, had put Rusk into third place and was edging up on Guthrie. Both the Norton and Guzzi outfits were operating outstation signalling systems. Woods, in fact, was using for the first time a highly comprehensive system he had devised years earlier and which actually gave him a much better service than his rivals'. Even so, Guthrie got the message and on his third circuit he sent the lap record up to 85.05 mph.

Rusk was still third and Duncan had climbed to fourth place. On his fourth tour Guthrie stopped for fuel and lost the lead temporarily to Woods. But he was back in first place on the fifth lap and, riding No 1, he began his last circuit 26 seconds ahead of the Dubliner. Nobody dreamed that Stanley could make up *that* difference, especially as it was expected that he would have to stop for fuel. Indeed, it was seen that his pit attendant was making ready to tank up the Guzzi. By the time Stanley reached Governor's Bridge on his sixth lap, Guthrie was already on top of the Norton signal station at Ramsey Hairpin on the other side of the Island.

Convinced that Woods would have to stop, Nortons flashed a signal to Ramsey telling them to give their man an 'ease-up' sign. But Stanley didn't stop! He came screaming past the pits at well over 100 mph and it was too late to warn

Guthrie. He had already received the Ramsey message and was knocking off the pressure on the last 14 miles.

Stanley was haring into Ramsey when Guthrie crossed the line to receive a victor's welcome. Champagne was bubbling. Photographs of Jim as the winner were on the way to London by air.

But then the scene began to change. Somebody phoned through from The Bungalow to say that Woods had almost obliterated that 26-second margin. Guthrie had started No 1; Woods was No 30. To win Stanley would have to finish less than 14½ minutes after Jim. Could he do it? Would the Guzzi, being driven well past the rev counter red line, hold together? Would there be another of those agonising empty-tank push-ins from Hillberry?

No 30's 'clock' finger snapped to 'C' for Cregny-Baa. Everyone with a watch was making furious calculations. It was impossible, they almost all agreed. But when the red lamp signalled No 30 at Governor's Bridge the vote was split three ways. 'He's done it! He hasn't! It's a dead heat!' cried the crowds, but when the scarlet Guzzi thundered over the line none of them really knew. However, in the timekeepers' hut there was no uncertainty and out came the message: 'Woods is the winner — by four seconds'!

The result caused a sensation. Admiration for Stanley was equally proportioned with sympathy for Jim. The latter's 'take-it-easy' last lap (nine seconds slower than his sixth) cost him a race he should easily have won. And the only fuel that Woods had left was in his Guzzi's float chambers!

Woods's last lap record speed was 86.53 mph —in a time of 26 minutes 10 seconds, and 72 seconds better than the previous best registered by Stanley himself during his 1933 Norton victory.

Though pipped at the post, Nortons lost no face in the 1935 Senior. Guthrie, Rusk and Duncan gave a superb demonstration of high speed reliability, finishing second, third and fourth, and for the third successive year both Manufacturers' and Club team prizes were won on Norton machines.

Then it was off to the Grand Prix circuits where Norton team men came first in both the 500 and 350 cc classes of the Swiss, Dutch, German, Belgian and Spanish events, finishing with the 'Ulster' where Guthrie gained one of the most thrilling victories ever witnessed in this always exciting race — which it so happened that year

carried the title of European Championship.

Guthrie and Rusk were mounted on 500s; 'Crasher' White had a 350. The Scot and the Ulsterman immediately went into the lead with standing-start laps at over 93 mph that annihilated all records.

On the second lap Rusk overtook Guthrie on the corner at Aldergrove but he braked too hard on some melting tar, skidded and crashed right in Guthrie's path, bringing Jim down with him. There followed a hectic sorting out of men and machines. Rusk had to retire but Guthrie was able to straighten out a twisted mudguard and pushed off again with footrests, gear control, handlebar and front wheel rim all bent!

The crash had dropped him to fourth place at the end of the second lap, but the indomitable Scot regained the lead with an incredible 95.35 mph lap, and from then on he kept well ahead of the field, finishing 3½ minutes in front of the second place man and setting up a world record average speed for a motorcycle road race at 90.98 mph.

When the 1936 season began there were many rumours that Norton had a supercharged multi-cylinder model on the stocks. If so, it was not forthcoming. What they did have was a much-modified single cylinder engine and a new frame. The latter had a straightforward plunger spring arrangement for the rear wheel, without hydraulic or other damping, and on the girder front fork the spring was supported on ball joints.

Engine-wise, full use of the allowable cubic capacity was made by revising the bore and stroke dimensions. An extra 0.7 mm bore diameter raised the capacity of the 500 model to 499 cc, while 73.4 mm × 82.5 mm produced 349 cc for the Junior. A greater cooling area was arranged around exhaust and inlet ports and twin-spark magnetos were fitted. Front brake diameter was raised from 7 to 8 in.

In the manpower department there was also a significant development. The official team of Guthrie, Rusk and White was strengthened by the addition of a quiet, unassuming lad from Grimsby, F. L. (Freddie) Frith, whose day-to-day work was that of a stone mason.

In alliance with race-wizard Nigel Spring, Norton-riding Freddie had crowned several years of distinguished Manx Grand Prix competition by winning the 1935 Junior event at race and record speeds. In the 500 cc class he had led for five of the six laps, losing by only 40 seconds to another Norton owner, Dr J. K. Swanston.

As TT time drew nigh Nortons' position looked somewhat doubtful. A broken arm had caused Walter Rusk's withdrawal and Jimmy Guthrie had crashed at the 11th Milestone during practising. However, doctors and masseurs had trimmed Jim back into shape and he was able to captain 'Crasher' and Freddie into a Junior TT situation that ended in a furore, with Guthrie again playing the leading part.

The Junior race opened in excellent weather and Jim at once produced his star performance, cracking record after record as he headed the field through four laps. To the great delight of his many supporters, new boy Frith followed closely, keeping ahead of the Velocette opposition spearheaded by Ernie Thomas and Ted Mellors. 'Crasher' White lay fifth.

With half the distance covered there was only one second between Guthrie and Frith; Thomas was 20 seconds behind Freddie. The fifth lap completely upset the applecart. At Hillberry Guthrie shed a chain. Quickly he refitted it but, so the story went, he had the help of a marshal when re-starting. The incident was reported to race HQ and the stewards thereupon disqualified the Scot, although he continued to ride. So the lap-five leaders were posted as Frith, Thomas, Guthrie, Mellors, White and H. E. Newman (Velocette).

Thomas dropped back after a tumble at Quarter Bridge and the position after six laps was Frith, Guthrie, Mellors, White and Thomas.

'Crasher' got the signal to press on and after a neck-or-nothing ride he overhauled Mellors so, with Guthrie ousted, the official finishing order was Frith and White ahead of Mellors and Thomas.

In his first TT Frith had won by 5½ minutes. The lap record, standing to Guthrie's credit at 80.11 since 1934, was broken five times—twice by Guthrie and three times by Frith, whose fifth lap average was 81.94 mph

At the prize distribution that evening the stewards reported that they had been mis-informed about the Hillberry incident, but they could not disturb the finishing order, although they allowed Guthrie's protest. They recom-mended that the value of the prize attaching to second place, which Jim would in all probability have occupied, be granted to the entrant.

Despite this extraordinary ruling, Guthrie, Frith and White were the trio who gained for Norton both the Manufacturers' and the Club team prizes.

The deposed Scot re-established himself in the Senior after a magnificent fine-weather, race-long scrap with Stanley Woods (Velocette) in which the lap record was broken three times—first by Guthrie on lap three, again by him on lap five, and then by Woods on lap six at 26 minutes 2 seconds—86.98 mph.

Everyone was expecting a last lap sensation such as had occurred in 1935, but just when he needed it most Woods's engine developed a bout of misfiring and Guthrie steamed home to win by a clear 18 seconds. His last lap time of 26 minutes 22 seconds included a second stop for fuel. The final order, Guthrie, Woods, Frith and White, had not changed throughout the race which had been such a punishing one that only ten of the 20 starters finished, three of them Norton private owners.

For the fourth successive year, Norton machines won both team prizes, and the Manu-facturers' award, having been won outright, was re-presented to the ACU by Bill Mansell. Norton motorcycles had now won 16 TT races and only once in six consecutive years had the company failed to bring off the Senior/Junior double.

On the Continent there was again a string of Norton 'firsts', but in the Ulster Grand Prix the clockwork regularity of the team suffered a set-back. Guthrie and Frith were the 500 cc con-tenders; for the 350 class 'Crasher' White was paired with a newcomer to Joe Craig's stable—H. L. Daniell. Londoner Harold Daniell was no stranger to Norton machinery. His first Island appearance had been in 1930 when he rode his own CS1 model in the Manx Grand Prix. Later he had been recruited to the AJS factory team.

Helped by his 'tunesmith' brother-in-law, Steve Lancefield, he had made his mark in the long-distance Isle of Man and Irish events and in numerous short-circuit races, notably at Crystal Palace.

Guthrie, who had covered a lap at over 96 mph in practice, was out of the Ulster race on the first lap, but Frith kept command of the 500 cc class, working up to a lap at 95.23 mph. After this he settled down to a steady 90, winning at 92.00 mph. Norton private owners J. W. Beevers and W. G. Wright were second and third.

Daniell and White were well ahead in the 350 cc class when Harold had to retire after a cable nipple breakage closed the carburettor airslide. White crashed when in the lead, having set the last lap record at 92.13 mph—then an almost un-believable speed for a 350 machine.

Chapter 15

The 'Double Knocker'

THE GERMAN TERM for 'cam' is *Knocke*; for 'twin cam' it is *Doppel Knocke*. So, when in 1936 Velocette produced a twin-camshaft engine, their racing engineer Harold Willis, who made a speciality of inventing descriptive motorcycling terms, naturally called the new type a 'double knocker'.

The first Norton double-knocker gear arrived for the 1937 season—applied to both 350 and 500 cc works engines. It was mounted on a cylinder head having finning that looked square in plan. Valve springs were not enclosed; port design had not been interfered with; bigger megaphones were fitted; and the brakes had been re-designed with cone-shaped hub shells.

With these machines Jim Guthrie, Freddie Frith and 'Crasher' White were factory-entered in the TT. Jack Williams was issued with an experimental mount which had the works pattern plunger sprung frame carrying a single-camshaft engine with enclosed coil-spring valves.

In practice, however, the dohc gear was found unsatisfactory and was changed for the proven (since 1935) single-cam rocker box with small 'tappets' between the enclosed rockers and exposed valve stems. The substitution was kept quiet and did not come to light until 1974 when Freddie Frith told me about it.

Run in excellent weather, the Junior saw yet another Norton 1-2-3 with Guthrie leading throughout, averaging 84.43 mph. He finished more than 2¼ minutes ahead of Frith, who was nearly 2 minutes ahead of White. The lap record was broken repeatedly by Guthrie, Frith and Woods (who was fourth on a Velocette), and was finally shared by Jim and Fred at 85.18 mph. Harold Daniell, racing a Norton for the first time in a TT, was fifth. Twelve of the first 18 finishers rode Nortons and both Manufacturers' and Club awards were won by the factory trio.

The 1935 Senior had been regarded as just about the ultimate in excitement that a TT fan could reasonably expect. That last lap duel when Woods beat Guthrie by a mere four seconds could surely never again be matched for sensation. But what happened two years later is still recalled, by those who had the good fortune to watch the 1937 Senior, as a peak in motorcycle racing drama.

The fact that Nortons had convincingly belted the opposition in the Junior was by no means regarded as an omen for a repeat performance in the major race. For one thing it was generally believed that there had been more than a little 'foxing' during the practice period and that none of the principal contenders had come anywhere near revealing true form. Then there was the 'foreign menace'. A Guzzi wide-angle twin, similar to the one which had carried Woods to victory in 1935 and therefore a proven 'quickie' was in the hands of a man who seemed well capable of using all the speed it could give him —Italy's champion, Omobono Tenni. Also, the BMW which Jock West was riding already had a reputation for tremendous power plus reliability.

But Nortons' chief challenge undoubtedly lay in the combination of Stanley Woods and the new 495 cc two-camshaft Velocette.

After the first lap Nortons' condition looked, as the hospital bulletins say, 'comfortable', the race leaders being Guthrie, Frith, Woods, West, White and Daniell, with Tenni seventh.

On the second tour Woods had passed Frith and a repetition of the 1935 dice was in full flight. With records cracking like fireworks, the Norton-Velo battle continued through laps three and four when, after the refuelling stops, the order was Guthrie, Woods, Frith, West, White and Tenni. Almost anything could happen—and immediately it did!

On the fifth lap, powering his way through the S-bend then known as 'The Cutting' just above the Gooseneck, Guthrie suddenly lost all his steam; his engine had blown up irrevocably—and Woods went into the lead.

Urgent 'all-out' signals were flashed to Freddie Frith, who already knew that his team's leader was out of the race and that it was up to him. Woods's complex signalling grapevine was also at work and the Irishman was hell-bent to keep ahead.

Can you picture the scene at the Grandstand when the sixth lap times were posted up? Frith and Woods were level-pegging in first place at a record average of 87.88 mph! The situation for both camps was agonising. For Velocette everything hung on Stanley; their second string, Ted Mellors, was way back in fifth berth behind

Nortons' White and Daniell, who themselves were too far behind the leaders to challenge Woods should disaster overtake the flying Frith. West, suffering from a leaking tank, had dropped to sixth place, the position occupied by Tenni when he retired on the fifth lap.

So into the last lap they went, neck and neck on time. Frith hurled his machine round the Island in a superb risk-all-or-nothing final fling — and came up with the TT's first over-90 mph lap— 25 minutes 5 seconds, 90.27 mph—to carry away the Trophy at a record race average of 88.21 mph, 2½ mph up on the previous year.

For Stanley came the bitter experience which Jim Guthrie had suffered two years earlier. Riding No 4 the Irishman finished, at 88.09 mph, while Frith (No 24) was still coming down the Mountain. For ten minutes the outcome was in the balance— but Fred brilliantly over-rode the hazards of Hillberry, Signpost Corner and Governor's Bridge, and swept across the line with a margin of 15 seconds!

Frith and Woods were the first riders to complete seven TT laps in under three hours. White in third place was approximately 8½ minutes behind the leaders. Mellors, Daniell and West completed the leader board and the Norton-mounted private owner from South Africa, Johnny Galway, was seventh. Of the 17 finishers Norton provided seven — two being on 350s, one of whom was Jack Williams who had ridden his experimental model into tenth place in both Junior and Senior classes. Of only seven riders who gained silver replicas, four were using Nortons.

Freddie Frith's marvellous victory brought the Senior Tourist Trophy to Bracebridge Street for the sixth time in seven years. In that period Norton motorcycles had filled no fewer than 17 of the 21 first three places in the Senior race.

That 1937 Senior stands as a landmark in the TT saga. It is especially remembered as Jim Guthrie's last Island ride and for the breakthrough of the '90' barrier. How many remember, or even know, that before he blew up, Guthrie had already lapped within three seconds of that amazing speed?

Through the summer 'Circus' tour the Bracebridge Street boys collected their customary laurel garlands with a particularly notable success in the Swiss GP which was that year's European Championship. Guthrie and Frith were the two works riders and they were first and second respectively in both Junior and Senior events, Frith raising the 500 cc record to 91.49 mph. It was the seventh successive year that Nortons had achieved the 'double' in this event and from it Guthrie emerged

as the Junior and Senior Champion of Europe.

Last fixture on the continental calendar of major races was the German Grand Prix, scheduled for Sunday August 8 on the tricky, twisting Hohenstein-Ernstthall circuit near Chemnitz in southern Saxony.

Now deeply involved in international motor sport, the Germans were pinning high hopes on their BMW, NSU and DKW riders, and to help counter this Nortons added Harold Daniell to the strength. In the Junior, Harold and 'Crasher' White had little difficulty in finishing first and second in that order, both riders breaking the course and lap records.

Right at the start of the Senior, Frith's machine began misfiring and it was left to Guthrie to fight it out with Germany's leading men, headed by Karl Gall (supercharged BMW). Jim had a poor start but soon established a comfortable lead and he settled down to lap steadily at around 84 mph. His third successive German GP win was in sight when on his last lap he entered the difficult Noetzhold Corner, not a mile from the finish line where the Union Jack was ready for hoisting. Spectators peering down the course were astonished when Gall and Kurt Mansfeld crossed the line, and it was not until the next finisher, Karl Bodmer, reported that Guthrie had crashed that news of the disaster reached the Grandstand.

For nearly 40 years it was generally believed that a locked wheel or a skid in loose sand caused the accident. Only in 1975 did I learn from Jim's mechanic, Bill Mewis, the real cause—a broken rear axle due to weakness in the plunger system. Gallant Jimmy Guthrie had fractured his skull and he died a few hours later in a local hospital. The shock of his death reverberated around the world for this modest, kindly Scot had won admiration wherever he rode.

As a mark of respect for his memory, the Norton works entries were withdrawn from the following weekend's Ulster Grand Prix. But work went on in the experimental shop at Bracebridge Street. Although it was generally believed that future racing success lay with multi-cylinders and supercharging, Joe Craig held on doggedly to the well-tried Norton formula—a robust, reliable, unblown single-lunger.

Using twin camshafts for his 1938 engines, the 'Professor' turned nearer still to 'square' cylinder dimensions. The 350 unit he changed from 73.4 mm × 82.5 mm to 75.9 mm × 77 mm. The 500 was altered to 82 mm × 94.3 mm. He left the valve gear practically untouched, but to cope with the extra power (52 bhp at 6,500 rpm) he stiffened up the 'bottom half' considerably, sinking the barrel $\frac{3}{4}$ in deeper into the crankcase mouth. Bigger cylinder fins were used and vertical finning was cast on to the front face of the crankcase.

The base of the lower camshaft drive bevel box was reshaped to allow a raising of the exhaust pipe for better cornering. Truly enormous megaphones were fitted. A remote-needle type Amal carburettor was flexibly attached to the inlet port.

For these potent motors a much stiffer frame was evolved. The long-familiar below-engine cradle was abandoned and instead two tubes ran continuously from the foot of the front down tube to the rear axle. Bracing struts, located just ahead of re-designed spring units, joined these tubes with the seat stays. At the front were telescopic forks which, contrary to general belief at the time, were not damped in any way. Modifications to strengthen the cone-shaped hubs were also made.

Only one of these machines—a 500—was ready in time for the North West 200 and it revealed little of its capabilities, for its rider, Frith, retired early in the race, having fallen on a patch of wet road.

Even at the TT the new 'bangers' were late in arriving and the practising period was half consumed before the Norton trio of Frith, White and Daniell got chances to try their latest mounts.

In the Junior the 'Joe motors', as they had already been nicknamed, impressed more by their reliability than by their speed. Stanley Woods and Ted Mellors had held their Velocettes first and second throughout the race and Freddie, 'Crasher' and Harold maintained station behind them, Fred missing second place by only seven seconds. Both the Manufacturers' and the Club team prizes were awarded to their entrants, the former going to Norton for the fourth successive year.

Despite their somewhat unpropitious Junior, Nortons were favourites for the Senior. The German blown BMW threat had been punctured when their top rider, Karl Gall, had to go to hospital after a crash while carrying out carburation tests on the Mountain. His compatriot, Georg Meier, a comparative newcomer to International road racing, had shown good form in practising.

In the event, Meier got no further than the foot of Bray Hill. While changing a 'soft' plug after the preliminary warming-up period he had stripped the thread in the cylinder head. He started on one pot and promptly retired. BMW hopes therefore lay with Jock West.

Once again the leader of the opposition was Stanley Woods with his Velocette. And what a battle he made of it! For the first two laps he chased Frith so closely that an ultra-quick fuel stop put him at the head of the race. Through laps three, four and five the order was Woods, Frith, Daniell, White, West and Mellors (Velocette). When the fifth lap times went up Frith and Daniell were level-pegging and Stanley was just three seconds ahead. It was on this lap that Fred set up a new record of 90.44 mph, thus beating his own 1937 record. But this was soon shattered by Harold Daniell who took the lead on lap six with a first-ever under-25-minute lap—24 minutes 57 seconds.

The last lap was an epic. When Frith (No 1) reached The Bungalow, Daniell (No 15) was at Ramsey and Woods (No 30) had passed Ballacraine. Five seconds covered them on corrected time and the intervals on real time were 7 minutes between Frith and Daniell, $7\frac{1}{2}$ minutes between Daniell and Woods and therefore $14\frac{1}{2}$ minutes between Frith and Woods.

Fred finished with his fastest lap of the race at 25 minutes 2.8 seconds. Then Daniell roared in with another cracker—24 minutes 52.6 seconds—91 mph! Stanley made a desperate over-90 mph last effort that pipped Frith by just two seconds.

It was Nortons' 19th TT success and they won the Manufacturers' team prize for the fifth time in six years.

Competition on the Continent was hotting up that year and Bracebridge Street riders had to fight hard for their laurels. In the European Championship (the German GP) White won the Junior. Daniell took both classes in the Swiss GP, while at the Belgian GP 'Crasher' White collected another Junior first and Frith was second in the Senior. In the Junior classes single-camshaft engines were sometimes used, for the 350 dohc motors mysteriously failed to match the degree of improvement achieved by their bigger brothers.

At the end of the season Bill Mansell called a press conference at Bracebridge Street and announced that Nortons were refraining from racing for one year. The astonished journalists were shown an order book, certified by chartered accountants, that revealed heavy commitments for the production of standard machines, a large part being in military contracts. Mansell was adamant. It didn't mean, he said, that Norton was out of racing for good. Experimental work would continue but for the next 12 months the company would not be entering competitions.

A further shock arrived in January 1939 when Joe Craig announced that he was leaving Bracebridge Street and transferring to Small Heath to become development engineer at BSA.

Throughout the winter and spring there were

rumours and speculation. Was the TT dead? Would there be an entry sufficiently adequate to support another Island series? The ACU remained outwardly unperturbed. There would be no changes in the regulations. Entry forms were being sent out as usual. Details and pictures were published of a supercharged 500 cc Velocette twin and of a supercharged AJS four.

In spite of the tricky international situation two German firms, BMW and NSU, said they would be sending TT machines. NSU had engaged 'Crasher' White.

In May it was learned that Freddie Frith and Harold Daniell, who had made plans to ride ordinary Manx-type Nortons, were to have the loan of their 1938 Junior and Senior 'bangers'. 'No sense', said Bill Mansell, 'in letting them gather dust.' Race entries by this time were up to 150 but only three British makers were giving official support—AJS, Velocette and CTS.

Frith led Woods (Velocette) up to lap three in the Junior race but the Norton began to lose power. Daniell was lying fourth having taken a toss in Ramsey. When Frith retired with a dead engine at Ballaugh, Daniell was close behind Woods and was eventually beaten from first place by only eight seconds. It was Stanley Woods's tenth TT victory—five of which had been achieved on Nortons.

On the day after the Lightweight race a hugely attended ceremony was held at the point on the circuit known as 'The Cutting' where Jimmy Guthrie had retired in his last TT, the 1937 Senior. The Guthrie Memorial was unveiled by the Island's Lieutenant-Governor. The view across Ramsey Bay looks towards Jim's native Scotland where, in his home town of Hawick, the people have a statue of their brilliant hero.

There were 47 starters in the Senior race and the BMW supercharged twins of Meier and West went straight into the lead, followed by the singles of Frith and Woods (Velocette), and that was the order at the finish. Daniell had retired with engine trouble. None of the leading British riders seemed able to repeat their 1938 speeds. Meier raised the race average slightly but Harold Daniell's magnificent lap record of 91 mph of the previous year was never in danger of being broken. Indeed it was to stand unscathed for 12 years until in 1950 a new Norton star, Geoff Duke, hoisted it to over 93 mph!

Chapter 16

Development through a decade

AS A CHANGE from racing, this chapter takes a look at the way in which the Norton production motorcycle developed through the decade from 1930 to the outbreak of the Second World War, when the sale of civilian models was halted. It should, of course, be borne in mind that the company followed the long-standing practice in both the car and motorcycle industries of announcing new models, issuing new catalogues and adjusting prices at times coinciding with the annual Shows. Thus the 1930 range was actually in being and on sale some two or three months before the end of 1929. It included a couple of two-port ohv machines, added in response to the then popular demand for duplicated exhaust systems. These were, in effect, variations of the models 18 and ES2 and were designated respectively the 20 and 22.

All the ohv engines were given full enclosure for the push-rods and the side-valvers had cover plates shrouding the springs, stems and tappets. A new type of silencer, parallelogram-shaped with a fishtail, resembling the 'Brooklands can', had been introduced, as well as chromium plating. Tank-side gear levers were optional to the regular footchange.

The CS1 and CJ models featured the type of camshaft and magneto drive that was developed earlier by Arthur Carroll for the TT engines. A noticeable difference between the two machines was that, whereas the CS1 followed the rest of the range in having its exhaust system on the nearside, the CJ's pipe was on the right.

Also available, as a 'special order job', was a Norton dirt-track machine, powered by a two-port 490 cc push-rod unit in a cobby frame with Harley-Davidson 'Peashooter'-type telescopic front forks. Built for use with dope fuel, it was supplied with a spare piston suitable for petrol-benzole.

The slump which followed the 1929 Wall Street crash had caused Norton to drop its prices considerably. For 1930 the 16H was listed at under £50, and £5 had been knocked off the cost of the CS1. During the course of the same year the company name, Norton Motors (1926) Ltd, was changed back to Norton Motors Ltd.

A most important change was made for 1931 when the long-familiar 'garden gate' frame was discarded for a pattern much lower in saddle height and much shorter in the wheelbase. Norton-made front forks with a central compression spring were standardised on all models and the net result was such a big improvement in steering and handling that the name 'Roadholder' was coined. Only the CS1 and ES2 types retained the triangulated rear torque tube arrangement.

In the engine department, magnetos, throughout the range, were located behind the cylinder, and dry sump lubrication was generally adopted. The side-valve motors were given detachable cylinder heads. A new style of bulbous petrol tank appeared and a four-speed gearbox was optional at £2 extra for the models 16H, 1, 18, 19 and 20.

Making their first appearance for 1932 were two mounts that were to become famous racers—the International models 30 (490 cc) and 40 (348 cc). Based largely on the existing ohc machines, they were supplied with racing equipment. The specially tuned engines had crankcases and rocker boxes in aluminium alloy and the inlet ports were offset and downwardly inclined. Close-ratio four-speed gearboxes had a semi-positive system of foot control. Large capacity chrome-plated fuel and oil tanks enhanced the all-round good looks of these pioneer production racers. The larger machine was listed at £90, which included a rear guard pad, ribbed front tyre and flexible petrol and oil pipes. The remainder of the range was hardly altered, though the CS1 followed the CJ in having its exhaust pipe on the offside.

A further improvement in Roadholder qualities was made for 1933 when the Internationals were fitted with TT-type rebound springs on the front forks. Four-speed gearboxes were standardised except for the side-valve machines which could be so fitted for £2 extra. The model 19, for so long a wonderful performer in the 600 cc class, had its 588 cc capacity increased to 596 cc by a 'squaring' of its bore and stroke dimensions from 79 mm × 120 mm to 82 mm × 113 mm.

The next season brought no major changes. Rebound fork springs came to all models, as did an oil-bath primary chain-case. High-level exhaust pipes could be fitted if wanted.

In 1935 the silencer became tubular and handlebars were rubber mounted. The Internationals acquired hairpin valve springs and these two models could be bought as out-and-out racers with engines hand-built in the racing department, straight-through exhaust pipes, TT-type gearboxes and a variety of extra equipment such as a special alloy cylinder head, $4\frac{1}{2}$ gallon fuel tank, tank-top chin pad and so forth. Also offered, at £5, was a reliability trials conversion 'package' for appropriate models—high ground clearance frame, raised exhaust pipe, folding kick-starter pedal, 'knobbly' tyres, trials gears and the like.

A general 'tidying up' was made for the 1936 season to give the road-going models a more 'solid' appearance. Bigger, deeper tanks were fitted; timing chests and magneto chaincase covers were given smoother, more rounded surfaces and the diameter of the push-rod enclosing tubes was increased. The ohc practice of using long cylinder head holding-down bolts, extending from rocker box to crankcase, was applied to all the ohv types, which had heavier, more widely pitched fins that not only lent a more substantial look but also reduced resonance.

There were no alterations to 1937 specifications but for 1938 the ohv engines had their push-rods inclined towards each other as they entered a redesigned rocker box that enclosed the valves completely. Side valves, too, were fully enclosed, with the springs and tappets working in a chest cast integrally with the cylinder barrel. A somewhat cumbersome, box-like silencer with two tail-pipes may have been effective but was not much admired. Plunger-type rear springing, as developed for the TT machines, was a £15 extra fitment for the Internationals.

Changes for 1939 mainly concerned price adjustments. Lucas Magdyno lighting and an electric horn were included in the quoted cost. The spring frame was made available for the ES2. Tubular pattern silencers re-appeared. International models to full racing specifications were being offered as complete machines with most of the previous 'extras', including rear suspension, embodied as standard equipment. Elektron was used for their crankcases; exhaust pipes ended in moderately sized megaphones. The price of the 490 cc International was £123 9s 6d and the 348 was listed at £115 19s 6d. The cheapest machine in the range in 1939 was the 16H at £61 5s, including electric lights. Just after the war this price had risen by well over £100, a large part of the increase being caused by Purchase Tax.

A label typed in red is pasted across the front of the Norton catalogue for 1940. It reads: 'NOT SENT OUT, DUE TO OUTBREAK OF 1939-1945 WORLD WAR II'. The 'range that never was' embraced 15 solo models, and four types of sidecar bodywork that could be fitted to the existing double triangulated chassis or to a new, simplified frame. In both cases the spindle was supported at its outer end and the third wheel was interchangeable with those on the machine.

Cradle frames were specified throughout the range. On ES2, 30 and 40 models the existing frame remained unaltered but on all the others a new form of cradle was employed in which the front engine lug was extended round the crankcase by means of two tubular members brazed to the gearbox bottom lug and bolted to the front engine lug.

The TT-type telescopic front fork was to be available as an extra on the ES2, 30 and 40 machines and on all models there was a gearbox modification to enclose fully the clutch operating mechanism and to bring the change lever into such a position that shifts could be made without the need for moving the foot from the rest.

A number of other changes included improved performance cams, a revised handlebar mounting, a central prop stand and better looking oil tank and tool box. Bigger diameter valve heads and carburettor chokes were introduced and aluminium cylinder heads on the side-valve engines replaced the cast iron units.

But undoubtedly the most interesting feature that would have altered considerably the characteristics of four of the most popular Norton mounts was a departure from the long-established 79 mm × 100 mm bore and stroke dimensions for the 490 cc side-valve and ohv engines. Had the Second World War not intervened the models 16H, 18, 20 and ES2 would have had 496 cc (82 mm × 94 mm) capacities, giving, so the aborted catalogue declared, 'enhanced performance and smoother power output'. It is strange that this innovation was not followed up after the war; for many years the Norton 500 roadsters continued with the old 79 mm × 100 mm formula.

Instead of the previous practice of supplying trials conversion kits for standard models, there were to have been 350 and 500 cc ohv mounts specially built with $5\frac{1}{4}$ in high ground clearance, short wheelbase frames, wide ratio gearboxes, high level exhaust pipes, knobbly tyres, lightweight front brake, raised handlebars, plated mudguards and so forth.

Telescopic front forks were part of the comprehensive standard equipment for the racing Internationals, the larger version carrying a price tag of just under £126 and listed with an engine of 499 cc.

Chapter 17

War and peace

THE LAST MAJOR race meeting of 1939 was the Ulster Grand Prix, in which Norton 'singles' played a secondary role to the supercharged 'multis'. This exceedingly fast circuit—incorporating the seven-mile Clady straight — gave great advantage to forced-induction engines and the long run of British machine dominance had ended in 1936 with Freddie Frith's Norton victory at 92 mph.

In the 15 years from 1922 to 1936 Norton riders had won the race 11 times — Joe Craig thrice, Stanley Woods four times consecutively (1930-33); the other winners were Hassall, Shaw, Guthrie and Frith. There had never been a foreign win. Then blown BMWs ridden by Jock West had taken the premier Trophy in 1937 (91.64 mph) and 1938 (93.98 mph). Nortons had abstained from participation in 1937, following Jim Guthrie's death.

Valiant efforts to match the supercharged foreigners had been made by AJS, with first air-cooled, and then water-cooled four-cylinder machines, and in 1939 it really looked as though they had a good chance. Joe Craig's announced transference from Bracebridge Street to BSA had never actually come about; instead he had gone to the AJS race development department in south-east London. The manufacture of AJS motorcycles had been moved from Wolverhampton to the Plumstead, near Woolwich, factory of H. Collier and Sons Ltd, makers of Matchless machines, after the brothers Charlie and Harry Collier had acquired the entire assets of A. J. Stevens and Co Ltd in 1931. By 1938 Colliers had become Associated Motor Cycles Ltd.

Craig had not been with AMC long enough to have had much to do with the production of the overhead camshaft V4 water-cooled supercharged models, but to ride one in the Ulster Grand Prix, in partnership with Bob Foster, he had signed on fellow Ulsterman Walter Rusk, and Joe was in charge of the race team that went to Belfast.

Walter Rusk was the first man ever to lap the pre-war Clady circuit at a three-figure speed—actually at 100 mph. But later in the race Italy's Dorino Serafini, after Rusk's front forks had broken, cut the Irishman's time by one fifth of a second, setting the record at 100.3 mph with the blown transverse in-line four-cylinder Gilera; his record average for the race was 97.85 mph. They

were records destined to stand for ever for the old Clady circuit, having been partly built over during the Second World War, was never fully used again. It was also Rusk's last race, for the Blond Bombshell was to lose his life while flying with the Royal Air Force.

So, as the summer of 1939 was ending, the long-threatened 'foreign menace' in motorcycle racing had established itself. A German on a German machine had won the supreme event, the Senior TT, and an Italian on an Italian machine had won the world's fastest motorcycle road race, the Ulster Grand Prix.

However, the Berlin/Rome axis was mounting a foreign menace of a very different kind. With the coming of September, when the Isle of Man boats should have been ferrying fans to the Manx Grand Prix, troopships were unloading the British Army on French soil.

*   *   *

'One in every four was a Norton' was the seven-word boast of Bracebridge Street, summing up six years of motorcycle production and representing over 100,000 military machines. In Navy and Air Force blue, khaki, camouflage and 'desert sand', 16H and Big Four solos and sidecar outfits played their war-time part in places all around the world. A considerable number of the combinations, especially those used in the North African campaigns, were fitted with a type of sidecar wheel drive that had been developed in the 1930s by Dennis Mansell for reliability trials work.

Looking back on those hectic years, when the emphasis was continually on more and more production, one tends to think that there would have been little time to spare for projects and developments other than those directly connected with the job in hand. Yet in 1944, when the war effort was probably at its highest level, the magazine *Motor Cycling* published details of a patent registered in the names of Norton Motors Ltd and C. G. Smith concerning a method of hydraulic damping for a telescopic front fork. In a comment on the layout, the paper's editor wrote that this was probably the first intimation for many people that the famous Roadholder forks, as used by Daniell and

Frith in 1938/39 races, were in fact not damped. About the same time another patent, registered by Norton Motors and Edgar Franks, who was on the company's technical staff, related to a snail-cam device for adjusting the rate of the springs in the plunger rear suspension. This arrangement was never put into production but the oil-controlled front fork became, of course, a standard feature of post-war Nortons.

The factory resumed peace-time production in August 1945 with just two types for the 1946 season—the 16H and the Model 18, priced respectively at £99 and £105, Purchase Tax being extra. Both machines had the full cradle frame hitherto used only for the ES2 and the ohc types. A general tidying up in appearance included a new, neater gearbox end cover similar to that which had been promised for the aborted 1940 range.

At the end of 1945 Bill Mansell, though continuing on the board, handed over the managing directorship to C. G. Smith. As a youngster straight from technical college, Gilbert Smith had joined James Norton's drawing office staff in 1916. Before becoming a director in the 1930s he had worked in practically every department in the factory and was steeped in the Bracebridge Street belief that Nortons were really the only motorbikes that mattered.

In 1946 Joe Craig re-joined the company as technical director.

Chapter 18

The September Series

THE MANX GRAND PRIX meeting of 1946 was such a memorable landmark in the story of motorcycle sport that, chronologically, this seems an opportune juncture for taking a look at the September Series which, like the midsummer TT, has seen Norton machines competing every year since the inception of the event.

The idea of a race on the TT course, under TT conditions, for ordinary amateur race enthusiasts, who had little chance of shining against works and dealer-sponsored stars, was conceived in 1923 by the Manx Motor Cycle Club. With the agreement of the Island government and the Auto Cycle Union, the Club set about organising what was called the Manx Amateur Motor Cycle Road Race Championship — for convenience sake generally shortened to the Amateur TT. In 1930 the title was changed to the Manx Grand Prix.

From the very start there was trouble over the definition of 'Amateur', and for several years the organisers struggled to find rules that would fully satisfy the intended spirit of the meeting. They did not want the competition to have any connection with 'the trade' and they were opposed to riders accepting help from manufacturers or 'bonus' money from accessory suppliers and suchlike.

At the first meeting the Club was strongly criticised because they refused to mention the names of the competing machines over the public address system. The race, said the officials, was for men — they did not concern themselves with the machines. In view of this determination to keep the Amateur free of the taint of professionalism, it seems strange that at first no objection was made to riders who had competed in the June TT events taking part in the September meeting. Among a number who did this was the winner of the initial Amateur race, held on September 20 1923, L. H. Randles, a Sunbeam exponent.

Five of the six Norton starters finished and the one who retired, R. O. Lowe, set up the fastest lap at 56.42 mph, having led for most of the five-lap race. It was a one-day affair, 350 and 500 cc classes being run simultaneously with a special trophy for the best performance in the smaller category. This method of running the race was retained until 1928 when the separate Junior and Senior two-day pattern was introduced. Randles repeated his 500 cc victory in 1924 when Norton were hardly in the picture. Fourth berth, as in the previous year, was their best effort. But the picture changed in 1925 when H. G. Dobbs headed a Norton 1-2-3. Another fourth place was the best registered for Norton in 1926 when the race distance was raised to six laps.

Then the Percy (better known as Tim) Hunt phenomenon arrived in 1927. This youthful Lancastrian, son of a well-to-do cotton spinner with sporting predilections, had been riding (surreptitiously for some years) motorcycles since he was 12. With a Model 18 Norton given to him as a birthday present in 1924 he had tried his luck at racing on the sands at Southport, with sufficient success to induce Mr Hunt Snr to buy him a new machine of the same type. This he entered for the 1927 Amateur. Under atrocious weather conditions he rode steadily into first place and made the fastest lap at 60.46 mph.

Recognising that his lad really had talent, Mr Hunt stumped up again and the new machine was a CS1 on which, after some more Southport gallops, Tim entered the 1928 Scottish Six Days Trial, winning a silver cup, the highest obtainable award. A month later he entered the same machine in the TT. On the third day of practising he fell off at the 33rd Milestone and so damaged himself that he was unable to ride in the race. Undeterred, and on Alec Bennett's advice, he filled in an entry for the September Amateur—a thing, as I have already said, which was allowable in those days. He also bought an ohv Levis (his first machine had been a two-stroke of that make) with which to contest the newly introduced Junior race.

If the Levis had not broken a valve at Creg-ny-Baa on the last lap, Tim would have won the Junior easily, for he had had a useful lead on every lap until the trouble struck. Incidentally, *Motor Cycling's* account of this event was the first of the many Island race reports which it was my eventual lot to write.

The Senior was run in excellent weather and Tim on his 'cammy' Norton came home a highly popular winner with a lap record at 71 mph that actually eclipsed anything that the June 'professionals' had so far achieved.

Sand races. the 'Scottish'. the TT and the

Amateur, all in six months, and all on this one motorcycle—how's that for a unique example of man-machine versatility?

An invitation from Walter Moore to join the Norton factory race team for 1929 was accepted and so Tim Hunt became the first of the long line of riders who graduated from the September Series to almost instant stardom in the big-time ranks. Thus recruited to the Norton stable were Harold Daniell, Fred Frith, 'Crasher' White, Johnny Lockett, Geoff Duke and Bob McIntyre, to name but half-a-dozen.

There were, however, some stalwarts who remained loyal to the 'Manx' throughout their racing careers. Without a doubt one of the most consistent of these was Yorkshire's Denis Parkinson who, from 1932 to 1953, contested 24 races (always on Nortons in the 350 and 500 cc classes). The reliability of his riding was remarkable; in only six races did he retire (one was a Lightweight event) and eight times he was among the first three. Having three times won the Lightweight event (on Excelsiors) he opted out of the 250 category. After his Junior Norton victory in 1948 he concentrated on the Senior and, having achieved his chief ambition with his 1953 win, he gave up riding to serve the sport as an official and a race commentator.

To go back to the opening paragraph of this chapter, the 1946 Manx GP remains a special occasion in the memories of those who participated because it was the first Island race that had been held since the Senior TT of 1939. The Manx GP of that fateful year had been cancelled with the outbreak of war and the ACU had not had time to set up the organisation for a 1946 TT.

Petrol rationing was the main difficulty. By various and devious means enthusiasts had been able to scrape together enough coupons to compete in some short course trials and pocket-handkerchief speed events, but the amount of fuel required for a full-scale long-distance IoM event, with its attendant practising, seemed to present an insurmountable obstacle. But not to the Manxmen, who were determined to get racing back to their island. It was a hard struggle, but eventually a sympathetic Manx government was able to tell the organisers that sufficient 'pool' petrol would be available.

And so the great reunion came about. Only those fortunate enough to be able to say 'I was there' can appreciate the feelings we experienced as we stepped on to the Victoria Pier in Douglas, made our way through the town and there, on the Glencrutchery Road, found the Grandstand beflagged and the scoreboards freshly painted just as if there had never been a war. The Mansells were back in the 'Castle Mona'; the 'Peveril' housed the race office; and the Press boys thronged the 'Sefton'.

The crowd at the Grandstand which had assembled to watch the start of the first practice session was one of the largest ever seen and there was a horde of press photographers eager to capture the historic moment as the first rider to open the series pushed his machine into action. One cameraman, threatened by his editor with instant dismissal if he failed to get the picture, had fitted two large bulbs into his flashgun, and the resultant blaze was so effective that the astonished rider shot off into the half-light of the early morning so bedazzled that he hardly saw Bray Hill! The photographer, *Motor Cycling's* Alf Long, producer of many magnificent racing pictures, was to be known for ever more as 'Flasher' Long.

The outcome of the 1946 Manx, the pundits said, was pretty certain to be a Norton 'double' for, as always, the black-red-silver tanks predominated, and most of the stars returned from pre-war successes were Norton-mounted.

Favourite for victories in both the Junior and Senior was Londoner Kenneth Bills whose Manx Grand Prix experience went back to 1936 and who had pulled off the double in 1938. Other old hands aboard Nortons included Johnny Lockett, Tommy McEwan, Peter Aitchison, Denis Parkinson and Harold Rowell.

As expected, Ken Bills handsomely won the Junior race and Nortons filled all the first six places except fifth berth. But in the Senior Bills's expected double was upset by a newcomer from Eire, Ernie Lyons, who, in very bad weather, pipped the favourite on a Triumph twin—despite a broken frame.

Over the years Norton machines dominated the Manx Grand Prix entries. The 'off-the-peg' production racers appealed particularly to the enthusiasts for two prime reasons. One was the inbuilt high-speed reliability of the Bracebridge Street singles. The other was the fact that over a long period only Nortons were able to offer both 350 and 500 cc race machines. Where the regulations permitted the use of a 350 cc engine in a 500 cc race, two class rides on the same machine were possible—and many a Senior replica has been won with a 350 Norton. Alternatively, a 500 cc machine could be converted to a 350 more or less simply by changing the engine—and vice versa.

Thus it is that, as with the TT and many other events, the saga of the September races is packed with Norton history. No other make of machine or type of event has done so much to help aspiring enthusiasts to graduate to motorcycle racing fame.

Chapter 19

Post-war problems and projects

IT WAS IN JANUARY 1947 that Walter Mansell announced he was leaving Norton Motors and that his son Dennis was going with him. Yorkshire-born and Birmingham-trained, Mr Bill had been associated with the company since 1913 when, as I wrote at the beginning of this book, he joined the board after R. T. Shelley had acquired the business. He became managing director in 1927 and had intended to retire in 1939 but had stayed on for the duration of the war. Dennis, who entered the firm from school in 1925, had been a director since 1938.

With the Mansells went Bill Mewis who, when he wasn't working in the experimental shop, was either Dennis's sidecar passenger or a mechanic-cum-pit-attendant *par excellence*. All three men continued to meet at the Abingdon King Dick spanner and tool factory in Tyseley, Birmingham, over which, along with other Midlands enterprises, Mr. Bill presided.

On the departure of the Mansells, G. A. Vandervell and E. R. Shelley, both sons of Norton chiefs (C. A. Vandervell was still chairman), became directors.

With only a few months in which to set up his race shop, Joe Craig had little chance to do any developing for the 1947 TT. His main problem was to adapt the pre-war race machines to run on 'pool' petrol, which meant—among other things—dropping the compression ratio of the 500 cc engines from 11 to 7:1.

Only one of the old brigade, Harold Daniell, figured among the works entries; the others were all newcomers to 'Joe Motors', being (as might have been expected) Manx GP stars Ken Bills and Ernie Lyons, plus yet another Irishman, who had never hitherto tackled the Mountain Circuit, A. J. (Artie) Bell.

In the Junior race Bills was the only Norton teamster to finish—21st. In the Senior he retired and Lyons was a non-starter.

The Senior winner, Daniell, was well supported by Bell, who not only finished second but tied for the fastest lap honour with Velocette's Peter Goodman at 84.07 mph. Norton-mounted Ted Frend, later to become an AJS team man, was fourth.

An innovation for 1947 was the staging of a Clubman's TT for 'amateurs' riding stock machines. The 350 and 500 cc classes were right up the street for Norton International riders and on these marques E. E. Briggs had a comfortable win in the Senior and the redoubtable Denis Parkinson took the Junior prize. Eric Briggs went on to achieve a Norton 'double' in the following September's two Manx GP races.

The Clubman's TT series ended after 1956: throughout this ten-year period Norton machines were continually providing Island experience for men who were on their way up to the major races.

'Professor' Craig and his men battled to make what they could of the low-octane fuel. Engine vibration and frame breakages plagued them. Regarding the latter troubles, I am reminded, as after-dinner speakers like to say, of a conversation that took place when Joe Craig and I went to the Douglas harbour pierhead to meet a boat that was bringing from Belfast some of the Norton boys who had been competing in a pre-TT Northern Ireland event — the 1949 Skerries 100, I think it was. As the steamer was pulling up to the quayside, little George Morrison, from Ballarat, Victoria, waved a greeting from the ship's rail.

'Good race?' shouted Joe.

The Aussie shook his head.

'How's the bike?' the 'Professor' wanted to know.

'Busted frame,' George called back.

'Rough course?' asked Joe.

'Just a rough crossing,' was the wicked reply!

Nevertheless, Nortons pulled off a Senior 1-2-3 in 1948, after Tenni's Guzzi had frightened them with a spectacular opening that put the fastest lap speed up to over 88 mph. Bell, Bill Doran and Scotsman Jock Weddell were the Senior trio; Bell was third to a couple of Velocettes in the Junior.

The immediate post-war years were a frustrating period for most people, and not least for the racing boffins. Inferior grade petrol was not the only problem they had to contend with. There were difficulties in obtaining suitable qualities of materials, such as steels and alloys. Currency, trade and travel restrictions were other hurdles to be surmounted.

On the development side Joe Craig was, perhaps, better placed than some of his main rivals for he had, as it were, only to pick up the threads of an already race-proven design. At home AJS put their faith in the new parallel twin, double overhead camshaft layout that, because of its spiky-looking cylinder finning, had been nick-named the 'Porcupine'. This engine had been originally planned for a supercharger and getting the naturally aspirated version to come up to expectations posed many problems.

Similarly, abroad, BMW, NSU, Gilera, Guzzi and Bianchi were faced with the re-fangling of units that had made their pre-1940 reputations with forced induction systems.

By 1949, four years after the end of hostilities, the hated 'utility' substitutes and makeshifts were disappearing. Seventy-octane petrol was still the only available motor spirit, but by now engineers were coping with it. Bob Foster's fastest lap in the Senior TT on a Guzzi wide-angle twin was only just short of 90 mph and Les Graham would have had a clear race victory if his Porcupine's magneto drive had not let him down when he was barely three miles from the finish line. He manfully pushed it in to tenth place and even-

tually won that year's World Championship title.

As it was, Harold Daniell, freely admitting that the moral victory was Graham's, collected a Senior Trophy for the third time in 11 years. And a distraught AJS fan was heard to remark that 'if Nortons fell in a cesspit they would come up with a bar of chocolate'!

This left-handed tribute to Bracebridge Street luck could have been repeated in some of the years that followed—and probably its originator was not old enough to recall those earlier occasions, when it seemed that nothing would go right for the silver-tank teams.

Johnny Lockett made the Senior a Norton 1-2 while in the Junior, for the second year running, Artie Bell played third fiddle to Velocettes.

Tuner and carburation specialist Steve Lance-field had undertaken the preparation of the 1949 Norton machines which had been given two-leading shoe brakes and smaller-diameter wheels to improve navigation. Joe Craig's activities were with an entirely new project—a double ohc racing four-cylinder engine. What happened to this conception is still something of a mystery.

Another kind of 'multi'—a roadster twin—had appeared at the 1948 Earls Court Show in the range for 1949. This was the work of development engineer Herbert Hopwood who in 1946 had joined Craig's technical staff after much

An artist's reconstruction of the water-cooled, double overhead camshaft four-cylinder engine that was intended to power Norton racers in the early 1950s. Developed by an engineering team responsible for the original BRM racing car, it never appeared in public.

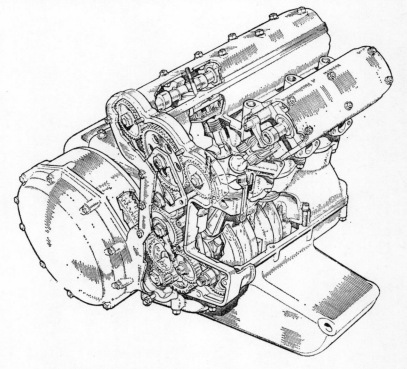

experience of twin-cylinder design with the Ariel and Triumph companies.

Using a frame, forks and gearbox typical of an ES2, the original Model 7 Dominator twin had an engine the basic concept of which has remained in the Norton catalogue right up to the present day, though it has, of course, grown in size and changed in shape. A vertically disposed, well finned, iron block flange-bolted to a sturdy crankcase, had parallel cylinder dimensions of 66 mm × 72.6 mm, giving a capacity of 497 cc.

Atop the barrels was an iron cylinder head embodying a pair of V-formed rocker boxes totally enclosing the ohv gear. Push-rods operated in a central, integrally cast inclined tunnel, at the base of which lay the transverse camshaft, located ahead of the cylinders. Forward of that was a separate dynamo and the magneto was situated behind the block. A triangular, smoothly polished timing chest cover enclosed the respective drives.

Backing up the Dominator at the 1949 Show were examples of the Models 16H, Big Four, 18,

ES2, 350 and 500 cc Internationals and the Manx 30 and 40 racers, the two last-named having double ohc engines for the first time. There was also a newly introduced 490 cc ohv trials mount, the 500T.

The display of silverware in addition to the Senior Tourist Trophy included the Senior trophies for the Clubman's TT and the Manx Grand Prix, both of which had been won during the season by a former GPO employee who had already become an acknowledged trials exponent —Geoffrey Duke, from St Helens.

While the Show was still in progress Duke, Artie Bell and Eric Oliver went on a record-breaking spree at the Montlhéry track near Paris. As a result, and in keeping with pre-war practice, the firm was able to announce before the exhibition closed that 21 world records had been captured by Norton.

As the year came to an end the FIM presented the World Championship awards, the sidecar class honour going to Eric Oliver.

Chapter 20

On the beach

AMONG THE FIRST THINGS that Gilbert Smith did when he took over the chief executive's office at Bracebridge Street was to make a study of the potential export market—particularly that part of it which embraced North America. In the course of the Second World War large numbers of US and Canadian servicemen had had experience of riding British motorcycles and many had, indeed, taken machines back home with them when they were repatriated. Consequently, orders for spare parts and inquiries for new mounts began to be received by English factories from across the Atlantic.

The States-side makers—represented by Indian and Harley-Davidson — built large V-twin machines. They had nothing to compare with the nimble, sporting and relatively lightweight British types. In a very short time our leading firms were renewing old contacts and making new liaisons with dealers and distributors from the Atlantic to the Pacific coasts. Gilbert Smith, true to the long-ingrained Norton precept that one of the most effective ways of proving the product is to demonstrate its superiority in open competition, surveyed the American scene with just that object in mind.

Of course it was Daytona that captured his interest. In the US National Championship event he saw America's supreme motorcycle competition, long established, hugely supported and carrying enormous prestige. To Gilbert's mind it was not really a race at all; at least it was not like anything else in the world of speed in which Norton machines were accustomed to shine. But it was, he recognised, *very* important. And so he went to work on it.

From regulations supplied by the organisers, the American Motorcycle Association, he gathered the main facts. A Daytona Championship meeting, held each March, was a two-day fixture with a 100-mile Amateur race on the first day and a 200-mile Experts event on the next. The course, along-side Daytona beach on the east coast of Florida, measured 4.1 miles per lap, half of it running south to north up the sandy beach, with the return half on a parallel seashore route of tarmacadam, the close turns at each end being artificially banked.

Mechanically, the requirements were rather similar to those for the Clubman's TT. Machines had to be made absolutely to stock specification and include a kick-starter. Compression ratio was limited to 7.5 : 1. This was enforced allegedly to prevent machines from going too fast, but it clearly favoured the 750 cc side-valve domestic machines. Furthermore, the standard issue of fuel was of 86 octane rating—too high a figure for the satisfactory operation of the current valve-in-head 500 cc engines. With such a low CR it was not possible to get them hot enough for optimum efficiency.

Norton had already scored one success in the Daytona series. In 1941, the last race to be held before the US entered the war, a Canadian, Bill Mathews, had taken the Championship. Otherwise each year from 1937, when the event was first held on the Beach (previously a course in Savannah was used), Americans on either Indians or Harley-Davidsons had always scored. The first post-war Experts race in 1947 had been won on an Indian.

But by the beginning of 1948 British machines were being used in North America in large numbers and for the Amateur of that year there were 37 British mounts, of which eight were Nortons, competing with a 'foreign' field of 76 Harleys and 48 Indians. In the Experts class the score was 19 Nortons, 18 other British makes, a BMW, 87 Harleys and 47 Indians.

With so many riders relying on the Bracebridge Street reputation it was no wonder Gilbert Smith thought it was 'very important', particularly as the Experts entry included the 1941 victor, Bill Mathews, again on a Norton and supported by Nortons' distributor for Canada and North America, Bill McGill, of Hamilton, Ontario.

Two single-camshaft 'Manx' models were prepared in Birmingham to suit the rules and were duly dispatched, one for Mathews and the other for a Detroit dealer-rider, Nick Pultorak. To look after these two mounts, as well as to give technical help to the other Norton riders, Smith engaged the independent tuner-engineer Steve Lancefield—who went to Daytona with virtually no knowledge of what to expect or how to cope with what he would find.

As it happened he was fortunate to make contact with a retired aeroplane manufacturer who put a splendidly equipped workshop at Steve's disposal, and the local Forestry Commission made available a flat four-mile unobstructed stretch of road for speed tests!

Having spent a large part of the pre-race period acclimatising his engines to unaccustomed fuel and devising ways to keep sand out of brakes and chaincases, Steve turned to look at the remarkable way in which the races were run. The pits, he found, were scattered along the sea-shore in no particular order and with no standardised form of identification, and little or nothing to keep at bay the vast numbers of spectators. Because of the enormous number of entries—around 170 in each race—riders were dispatched in bunches of 15 at six-second intervals and so lap scoring became a nightmare.

The rules allowed each rider four pit attendants —one for handling refuelling, one for oil topping, one to look after goggles and one general-purpose bod whose main task was to keep the depot clear of sightseers.

In the opening Amateur event, despite all these difficulties, nothing drastic went wrong for the leading Norton riders. Don Evans, still an 18-year-old schoolboy, was first with Dick Klamfoth second.

The first half of the Experts 200-miler went well for Nortons. Up at the front Canadian Bill Mathews was duelling with Indians' Floyd Emde, and Nick Pultorak was well in the picture, though the Norton boys were prone to spills on the turns. This was probably because the fitting of a kick-starter meant a very low bottom gear which they found difficult to engage. Indeed, after one toss, Mathews confined himself to three speeds only.

The race drama came when it was time to re-fuel. Emde made a rapid top-up in only 31 seconds, but when Mathews arrived things went sadly amiss. First he could not locate his depot. Then a pit attendant splashed fuel in all directions and, for safety, Mathews stopped his engine. (The rules permitted fill-ups with engines running.) Re-starting on wet sand lost more time, all of which amounted to a costly 65 seconds. Nevertheless, Mathews eventually finished second, only 16 seconds behind the flying Californian, Emde, whose average speed was 84.01 mph—4 mph up on the previous record. Mathews's speed was logged at 83.67 mph.

It took a long time to get the results sorted out, for even the officials weren't sure of their lap scoring and actually required the first three finishers to 'accept' the final findings. Mathews

was sure he had been robbed and produced a lengthy statement in support of his belief. However, the philosophic Steve, although convinced that Bill had won, told me when he returned to England: 'Without any effective lap scoring evidence of one's own, it was rather difficult to disagree! That is the American way of running a race. They like it like that, and it is not for visitors to say otherwise. One just has to learn by experience, and if I were to go again I should start at a much better advantage.'

Steve did not, in fact, return to Daytona. At the end of the season he took on, as recalled in the previous chapter, the job of getting the 1949 TT Nortons ready for the fray, and Gilbert Smith asked Francis Beart, about whom I shall be writing more later, to lead the next sortie to America.

More than ever determined to wring an Experts victory out of the Beach, Gilbert set things humming from Birmingham; directives, letters, memos and notes flew in all directions to oil, tyre and plug suppliers, shipping agents, insurance companies and, of course, to a large number of Norton friends across the Atlantic, for Beart's brief included a tour of dealerships.

Francis himself, in his customary methodical manner, went to work on the two single-cam Manx mounts earmarked for Bill Mathews and Dick Klamfoth, who had been upgraded to Experts status.

Forewarned with Lancefield's information and experience, Beart paid particular attention to re-fuelling methods and produced a highly efficient funnel-type of quick filler, and was not unduly worried about the haphazard pit arrangements that had prevailed in the previous years. The organisers had decided to erect barriers to confine the public and the pits themselves were sited in an orderly fashion near the south turn where riders would be travelling slowly anyway.

For his Daytona headquarters Beart was lent a fully equipped garage by a local resident, William Thomas. From Canada came ex-Norton rider Tony Miller and his wife to help with the lap charting and clock watching.

The Amateur entry list was made up of 91 American and 31 British machines, among them being 13 Nortons. It resulted in a Norton 1-2 with one of the most spectacular finishes ever seen in a race. Don Evans, the previous year's winner, had been having a furious battle with Ted Totoraitis and was so eager to make the last lap his fastest that he overslid the final turn and crashed into the man with the chequered flag. Neither was more than scratched and both Evans and Totoraitis averaged close on 80 mph—breaking the 100-mile record.

Riding strictly to Beart's orders, his two men, Mathews and Klamfoth, plus another Norton rider, Tex Luse, played a waiting game in the earlier stages of the Experts race, holding good positions close to the leaders of a field that included 73 Harleys, 42 Indians, 16 other Nortons, 21 further British bikes, one Guzzi and one BMW.

Around the 40th lap Beart put the pressure on and the order became Klamfoth, Mathews and Luse, and it remained thus to the finish. All three broke the previous record, Klamfoth's average being 85.21 mph.

News of this hat-trick — translated by the Americans into 'Stetson Sleight' — flashed round the world and complimentary cables showered on Beart and Bracebridge Street. Gilbert Smith's justifiable pride in seeing his determination fulfilled was royally crowned when he received a telegram from Buckingham Palace signed by the Duke of Edinburgh: 'Congratulations on your very fine achievement'.

It was with three double-knocker Nortons that Frank Beart returned to the Beach in 1950. Changes in the rules allowed 8.5:1 compression ratios and there was also a stipulation, made to counter the entry of 'factory specials', that machines could be 'claimed' and purchased after the race in the manner of a 'selling plate' on the Turf.

The Norton trio were Mathews, Klamfoth and Ernie Roccio, Tex Luse having been injured in an earlier event. Mathews got his revenge on Klamfoth and another Norton rider, Bill Tuman, finished third according to the lap checkers. But a protest was upheld and Tuman was eventually relegated to fourth berth, Roccio finishing seventh. Mathews's winning speed was another record— 88.40 mph. In the 100-miler Dick Curtnor (Norton) was second.

Back again in 1951, Beart's factory-sponsored charges were the Groveport, Ohio, farmer Klamfoth and another rider from Ohio, Bobby Hill. Other Norton riders for the Experts event were Don Evans and Dick Curtnor, both upgraded from the Amateur ranks. Klamfoth was uncatchable. Curtnor gave valiant chase until his pit crew spilled fuel during the fill up and his machine burst into flames. Beart, using his mathematically designed special filler (the pattern was used long afterwards), topped his mounts up in around 20 seconds each.

British machines, of which there were 56 (20 Nortons) completely dominated the race and, but for Curtnor's conflagration, it might well have been another 1-2-3 for Norton. As it was, Klamfoth and Hill finished well ahead, the winning speed being 92.81 mph.

A nephew of the Daytona veteran Ed Kretz Snr, Bob Panoma, had gained a Norton victory in the Amateur.

That was the last year Bracebridge Street sponsored Daytona riders and not long afterwards the AMA introduced new rules that prohibited the use of ohc engines.

In 1952, under very bad weather conditions which completely washed out the Amateur event, there was a Norton 1-2 in the Experts, Klamfoth winning at 87.77 mph. In the following year a Manx model won the Amateur, but a third place was the best Norton could achieve in the big race, which was won by a Harley-Davidson.

In the eight Daytona meetings held between 1941 and 1953, Norton riders had three times won the 100-mile race and twice been second. The tally in the '200' was five firsts, four seconds and two thirds. From 1948 to 1951, when the factory-sponsored machines were competing, the race speeds rose by almost 10 mph.

Chapter 21

On four wheels

A FRIEND of a friend of a friend persuaded Gilbert Smith to sell one of the circa 1953/4 works 500 cc racing models. The deal must have taken some putting through for it had always been strict Norton policy to keep the 'Joe Motors' out of private owners' hands—and when Gilbert found out what had happened to the machine he was furious. Anyone who ever encountered CGS when he was put out will know what that meant. His beautiful, virtually unique racing motorcycle had been broken up just to provide an engine for a small car!

It was at about this time that the sport of 500 cc car racing was at its peak. The cult had begun in a small way soon after the war when a group of enthusiasts started a movement to race simple built-on-a-shoestring vehicles, because the cost of construction and operation of real *bolides* was out of the question. The idea wasn't new. Back in the middle 1920s what was called 'plank racing' had been suggested and encouraged by the magazine *The Light Car and Cycle Car*. The 'plank' car stemmed from the small boy's contraption of a board fitted with four bicycle wheels. To this basic layout was to be fitted a motorcycle engine and the have-nots could go racing happily on next to nothing. A Cyclecar Club (later to become the Light Car Club) was formed, but the original 'plank' never materialised. Much the same thing happened to the post-war scheme for 'cheap' 500 cc cars (and also later to 'cheap' go-karts).

In 1946 the 500 Club was formed and there were some genuine attempts to construct a £50 skeleton that the originator of the project had prescribed, but in no time at all backyard racing had developed into a full-blown, highly organised business. The 500 Club became the Half-Litre Club (forerunner of the present British Racing and Sports Car Club) and 500 cc racing became Formula III, with International recognition. A part-time hobby meant for impecunious home constructors blossomed into commerce on a high financial international scale.

The first constructors were content with engines ripped from second-hand motorcycles and one of the sport's most outstanding builder/drivers, Reg Bicknell, has recorded how he lightheartedly started out with a set of alloy wheels and the bits of a 1933 single camshaft International Norton which he had bought for £30. Though the owner of a professional garage workshop, it took him two years before his original Revis car was ready to race.

Pioneers among those who went into Formula III in a business-like way, both as drivers and manufacturers, were the now-famous Coopers, Charles and his son John. And from the start of this enterprise Francis Beart was associated with them to tend the Norton engines which they used.

Beart's entry into half-litre car craft came in 1947 when his pre-war 490 Norton sprint motor was fitted into G. R. Hartwell's Monaco, built at Watford and used for hill-climbs and speed trials.

At Silverstone in 1948 R. M. 'Curly' Dryden, landlord of a Dorchester-on-Thames hotel and a highly successful driver, had the first car to be powered by a Manx twin-cam engine—Beart prepared.

These engines very soon began to appear in a variety of 500 cars. Of a dozen makes marketed in the 1953/4 period eight were available with double-knocker engines. A typical example was the Arnott Mk 1, a medium-priced model at £800 with a Manx engine.

These were good times for builders, tuners, drivers and track promoters, and not least for Nortons who were pressed to keep up with orders for complete engines and spare parts. At the height of the boom Beart, his manager Ray Petty and assistant Phil Kettle were handling six or seven units a week.

Francis was not the only specialist who put his Norton know-how at the disposal of the half-litre fans. Steve Lancefield was the man who tuned the Manx units that helped Kieft driver Don Parker to become Formula III champion in successive years.

For the 1953 season Beart designed and produced the Cooper Mk VII car which gained a clutch of records in 350, 500 and 750 classes, all collected in a Montlhéry outing. The drivers were John Cooper and Eric Brandon. With the 350 cc engine the best speed over the 50 kilometres distance was 105.71 mph; the 500 reached 118.03 over the same distance and the 750 (actually 502 cc) reached 119 mph. The Junior job put the hour record at 103.46 mph and the 500 averaged 117.26 mph for 60 minutes.

In 1954 the 'short stroke' 86 mm × 85.62 mm engine was introduced and these motors were hard to get. Mostly it meant buying the complete motorcycle and extracting the power unit. Beart's premises at Byfleet in Surrey became stacked to the ceiling with engine-less racing mounts!

Driving the Beart Mk VIIA Cooper in 1954 international meetings Stirling Moss collected six first places, two seconds and three lap records. In that season drivers using Beart-prepared Nortons bagged 96 firsts, 72 seconds, 57 thirds and 8 hill-climb and sprint records. Don Parker won the *Autosport* Championship and Stirling Moss the Light Car Trophy. Other outstanding Beart clients included Les Leston, Stuart Lewis-Evans, Reg Bicknell, Ivor Bueb and R. K. Tyrrell.

Over the next three years Formula III became increasingly cut-throat and expensive. Cars without either engine or gearbox were costing up to £1,000 and to be in the picture at all required an initial outlay of some £2,000—for a car and two engines, two gearboxes and two sets of wheels for wet and dry tyres.

At the same time spectator interest was beginning to flag. Promoters cut starting money and in 1958 the fairy godmother oil companies withdrew their financial support. The 'golden' days of Formula III were at their end.

Chapter 22

On the rough

SINCE THE BEGINNING of this century the world of motorcycle sport has come to include many kinds of organised competition: road and track races, hill-climbs, sprints, speedway, scrambling, moto-cross and reliability trials. And the 'odd man out' among that lot is the reliability trial, all the others being essentially speed spectacles with a strong crowd attraction. A trial is as different from the TT as a foxhunt is from the Derby.

Motorcycle endurance, or dependability tests began almost as soon as the machines came into general use. Speed restrictions on British roads prevented racing; an alternative for demonstrating mechanical reliability was the long-distance run, and the most popular of these was the 'End to End'—that is from Land's End to John o' Groats, or vice versa. So many pioneers undertook this arduous adventure that it developed into what almost amounted to record breaking, with speeds exceeding legal limits—so much so that the authorities took action.

But the idea remained firmly implanted that the best way to demonstrate motorcycle reliability, without a speed factor, was to subject the machine to long journeys, which included the stiffest kind of terrain and the steepest hills that it could reasonably be expected to surmount.

The motorcycle clubs began to convert their rallies and sedate social runs into competitive events which were called reliability trials. One of the leaders, and for a long time the foremost, of the organisations running these multi-mile events was the Motor Cycling Club which staged its first London to Edinburgh Ride in 1904. It involved night and day riding for 24 hours and all those who reached the Scottish capital—22 out of 46 starters—within the stipulated time limit received gold medals. The competing machines were quite standard roadsters and for some 20 or more years this was the general pattern of a British reliability trial, though in 1911 the Colmore Cup Trial set a new style with a one-day event.

The Edinburgh Club launched its still-going-strong series of the Scottish Six Days Trials in 1909, and in 1920 there began this branch of the sport's premier event, the International Six Days

Trial. It was in the latter event in 1926 that Phil Pike with his hack Norton outfit, as recalled in the earlier chapter on the Maudes Trophy, was a member of the team that won it for Great Britain.

'The secret of Norton success', sang the copywriters of those days, 'lies in the fact that standard machines are used in all events. The amateur has the same machines as are used by Nortons' own riders—and the same opportunities of success are his. A man who chooses a Norton motorcycle for ordinary use is therefore assured of a machine *capable* of passing any endurance test with flying colours.'

As substantiation of their policy Nortons published, year after year, long lists of private owners', as well as works riders' successes in trials, along with the road race and track victories.

It was in the latter half of the 1920s that a new type of trial developed, and it is a chicken-before-egg puzzle to determine what, or who, brought about the change that produced the specialised trials mounts.

By 1926 the previously popular, long distance 24-hour events, running mainly on public roads and kept strictly to a set average speed by means of time checks, were fading away. Nevertheless, open classics like the Colmore Cup and the Victory Trial continued to use courses that could be ridden by touring machines and, indeed, the 1926 Victory Trial was won by a car. But the old rules had just about done their job in fostering dependability. Motorcycles had become so reliable that the formula 'keep going and keep on time' no longer meant anything. A bit more ginger was needed.

One of the first trials to provide this was the Bemrose, which was organised by the Derby and District Club whose secretary, Fred Craner, was later to be the mainspring of the famous Midlands race circuit at Donington, alas, like Brooklands, a Second World War casualty.

The Bemrose novelty was called an Extraordinary Time Check, which meant that riders had to cover quite a long rough section in a given time. In the Peak District the Derby Club had plenty of off-road terrain available for the operation of an ETC, but elsewhere clubs without such facilities had to find some other means of sorting winners out of the increasing numbers of unpenalised performances that were occurring. The time-honoured practice of handing out gold medals to all who had clean sheets wasn't good enough for the publicity hungry manufacturers, who wanted nothing less than 'first and best' for their success advertisements.

Acceleration and brake tests, and combinations of both, were evolved and riders' performances were calculated on complicated formulae involving time and distance, constants, and square roots, so that regulations began to look like extracts from an algebra treatise.

It was these special tests that completely altered the pattern of trials at this time. Local authorities and police objected to the holding of acceleration tests on public roads (some of the tests were verging on blast-off sprints) and organisers were obliged to seek away-from-it-all sites—and so discovered an entirely new world of exciting trials country.

At the same time, the crafty competitors, realising that the ultimate destination of awards was depending more and more on special test performances, began adapting their machines expressly to cope with the new conditions.

Thus the situation snowballed. As the course planners moved away from the old-established routes so the going got tougher; concurrently the factory competition departments were raising ground clearances, re-jigging rakes and trails, gearing down and tuning up for maximum torque at low revs.

In the midst of all this came the competition tyre—the invention of G. B. Goodman, a member of the then all-powerful Norton trials team, which included Norman Hooton and Dennis Mansell. Graham Goodman, son of a safety pin manufacturer, got his first taste for trials riding when he used a Sunbeam in Birmingham University Motorcycle Club events. As an 'independent' he rode Nortons exclusively for some ten years, always brilliantly, whether solo or with a sidecar. The British Experts Trial—in which only the *crème de la crème* of trialsmen may compete—was his idea, but he never took part in it, preferring to supervise its organisation to ensure that it maintained the highest standard required of an event of such supreme importance.

His gift to the trials world, the 'knobbly' tyre, came about as a result of experiments he made with the ordinary roadster heavy duty covers then favoured for trials work. By cutting away large lumps of rubber from the treads he found his wheels obtained vastly improved adhesion in the mud, clay and sand that the route plotters were serving up as observed sections. The Goodman tyre was taken up commercially, and by 1930 was standard wear on trials mounts everywhere.

The mounts that Goodman, Mansell and company were using in those days were specially built up in the factory, not only to suit the riders' statures and personal requirements, but also specifically to contend with the various types of events and the going likely to be encountered therein. To obtain the tremendous urge needed to send a sidecar outfit rocketing non-stop to the summit of some fearsome gradient, Mansell often employed TT ohc engines tuned for alcohol fuel. He also pioneered sidecar wheel drive, but this afforded such overwhelming advantage that it was eventually barred in most open trials. During the years when Dennis Mansell was handling his Nortons he won practically every open award obtainable by a sidecar driver and when he retired the D. K. Mansell Trial for sidecars only was instituted in his honour.

It would be tedious, if not almost impossible, to make a list of all the successes garnered by Norton riders in reliability trials, but fairness demands that special tribute should be paid to a trio of Bracebridge Street stalwarts whose trials skill throughout the 1930s was of such a high order that they were frequently called on to join the British teams in International Six Day events: V. N. Brittain, J. Williams and H. J. Flook—their names pepper the pages of trials history. Vic and Jack were a pair of superb all-rounder soloists. Harold Flook was a dedicated, utterly dependable sidecar man whose sideboard must be bent double with the weight of the silverware he and his passenger wife accumulated during their long partnership on the trials courses of Britain and Europe.

As I mentioned in an earlier chapter, it was not until 1949 that Norton produced a purpose-built trials mount, the 500T. Before that, private owners mostly had three choices as regards machinery. They could use standard models, as did the pioneers; they could modify their machines to resemble as closely as possible those of the works riders; or they could order any model from the range with a trials specification of 'goodies' that included high ground clearance frames, special narrow forks, knobbly tyres, folding kick-starters and so forth.

The 500T (which could, of course, be supplied with a 350 cc engine) fitted the requirements of a trialsman of that period. Primarily he needed a robust, but not too heavy, powerful machine delivering plenty of torque at low engine revolutions. Few people then believed that anything under 350 cc was capable of winning a major trial and two-strokes were regarded as tiddlers needing an awful lot of leg work to aid their puny power outputs.

Aboard solo 500Ts riders such as Geoff Godber-Ford, Ted Breffitt, Geoff Duke, Johnny Draper, Jack Blackwell, Rex Young, Dick Clayton, Ted Ogden, Doug Crennell, and the Milner brothers, W. A. J. (Waj) and Roger, hauled in the prizes. While still combining rough riding with racing, in 1950 Duke won the Victory Trial, sandwiching it between his Clubman's TT/Manx GP double first and a Senior TT trophy.

A look at the results of the 1951 ISDT, held in Italy, shows how popular Norton trials machines had become. Of the 34 riders of 500 cc solos who gained gold medals, six were Norton-mounted—J. V. Smith, E. Wilson, P. Baldwin, J. E. Breffitt, R. B. Young and R. Clayton; the last three were Manufacturers' team prize winners and Clayton was also a member of the successful British Silver Vase team.

In the sidecar category of British trials, following in the wheel tracks of Mansell and Flook, Arthur Humphries, with his brother Harry in the 'chair', amassed a hoard of awards that included ACU Trials Drivers' Stars and 'premiers' in the British Experts and the Southern Experts Trials.

Bracebridge Street never listed a machine specifically intended for cross-country racing of the 'scrambles' type, which no doubt largely explains why the annals of that extremely arduous branch of motorcycling, international motocross, contain the records of practically only one consistently successful Norton rider — L. R. Archer. 'Young Les', so called because his road-racing father was also named Leslie, battled his Nortons round the British and Continental courses for over 12 years and he was twice named European Moto-cross Champion. Virtually independent of Bracebridge Street facilities, Les's machines were prepared and his engines tuned by his friend and mechanic Ron Hankins, and at the height of their prowess they constituted a formidable pair in a sport that is as tough on the machines as it is on the men.

The Model 500T Norton was first made in 1949 and the type carried many notable trials riders to success. This picture shows how it looked in the last year of its production life, 1954.

38: *Against a 1920 Brooklands background that clearly shows the steep Home Banking, the original Wizard of Speed, Daniel O'Donovan, poses with one of the BS side-valvers on which he set no fewer than 44 records, including the flying kilometre at 82.85 mph (see picture 8).*

39: *Albert Denly who, in 1927, raised the Hour record to 100.58 mph on a Spring-prepared Norton, here gets ready for a Brooklands race with one of the earlier ohv machines.*

40: *Brooklands 'cans' adorn the twin-pipe exhaust system of the 588 cc ohv Norton which George Tucker was racing in 1928.*

41: *One of the Brooklands Boys regularly successful on Beart Nortons was Denis Minett, pictured in 1938 with Francis (centre), after lapping the track at 104 mph on the 350 cc machine. The engine was a 1932 type with a bronze head and coil valve springs.*

42: *Seen through a window of Chronograph Villa, a mixed field of solos and sidecars lines up at the Brooklands Fork for a 1926 'Bemsee' Cup Day race.*

43: *The free way into Brooklands —under the banking and down the river—all under police supervision!*

44: *Great Britain's Trophy team Norton sidecar driver Harold Flook checks in for the August 1939 International Six Days Trial, held in Nazi-occupied Austria. The British teams abandoned the event at mid-distance when Germany invaded Poland.*

45: *With potent and beautifully prepared outfits, Dennis Mansell was hard to beat in the one-day classic trials during the 1930s.*

46: *Today's riders will scarcely believe that this was Nortons' Trials Model in 1947. Shortened wheelbase, 5½ inch ground clearance and wide gear ratios distinguished it from a standard roadster.*

47: (*Above*) *Most people associate Eric Oliver with World Championship Norton sidecars. In fact, he raced solos from the mid-1930s to the 1950s and here he is about to start practising for the 1947 TT.*

48: (*Above*) *The Beart Norton used by Denis Parkinson in 1948 to win the Leinster 200, the Hutchinson Hundred 350 class at Dunholme, and the Junior Manx GP, the latter at 78.20 mph.*

49: (*Left*) *At the start of the 1949 Senior TT the Duke of Edinburgh chats with the previous year's winner, Artie Bell. Machine No 4 is Les Graham's AJS Porcupine.*

50: (*Below*) *Another Manx GP success for Beart Nortons came in 1949 when Belfast's Cromie McCandless won the Junior event, with a record lap.*

51 and 52: (*Above*) *Nortons' 1950 1-2-3 team, Duke, Bell and Johnny Lockett, with Joe Craig, make a background for Geoff's machine which Graham Walker has just sampled on the Mountain Mile. (Right) Geoff Duke scores his first TT victory—in the 1950 Senior —chased home by Artie Bell. They both rode new-type Featherbed machines.*

53: *'The Duke' sails his Senior Norton over Ballaugh Bridge, on the way to his 1951 'double' and his third Trophy.*

54: *Post-race jubilation! 1951 Junior TT winner Geoff Duke links with runner-up Johnny Lockett (right) and third man Jack Brett. Immediately behind Geoff is his pit attendant, Dr Steve Darbishire, who teamed with Frith and fellow medic Swanston in Nortons' 1935 Manx GP 'double treble'.*

55: *First Norton multi since Rem Fowler's days was the 497 cc parallel-twin Dominator, introduced for 1949. This is the 1951 plunger-sprung version.*

56: *Crossing Ballaugh Bridge on his International model, Ivor Arber heads for a first place in the 1951 Senior Clubman's TT.*

57: *A revised exhaust pipe shape and a reversed cone megaphone were features of the 1951 Manx models.*

58: *Splitting the Gileras of A. Milani and Reg Armstrong, Ray Amm came a courageous second in the 1953 Belgian GP. His Norton has full finning around the cam driveshaft, oil-cooled exhaust valve and an offside rear brake.*

59: *Ray Amm with the 'kneeler' that made its appearance at the 1953 TT meeting and which, in modified form, later gained him the Hour record at 133.50 mph.*

60: *For the 1954 TT, Nortons used this curious form of wind cheater, nicknamed the 'proboscis'. Fuel was carried in the pannier tanks. This was Amm's Senior-winning mount, being Press-tested on the Mountain.*

61: *When not streamlined this is how the 1954 motors looked. Noticeable features are the outside flywheel, exhaust valve oil cooling, large flap-type breather on the crankcase front and the SU petrol pump driven from the inlet camshaft.*

Chapter 23

On the track

BEFORE THE SECOND WORLD WAR, for people in motoring sport the 'Track' meant Brooklands. And no other make of motorcycle was more closely associated with Brooklands than Norton. Had not the very first built-for-speed silver-tankers gained their fame as the BS models — the Brooklands Specials?

Today a man must be well over 40 years old to be able to say that he remembers a Brooklands race, for the track was never used for its original purpose after 1939, having been broken up and built over during the Second World War years.

But those who *can* recall the heydays of the famous Concrete Saucer will never forget it, for the place had a fascination uniquely its own. Montlhéry, Arpajon, Monza and the few other European 'speed bowls' never possessed the atmosphere, the camaraderie that permeated the Paddock. Nowhere else could a man experience the thrill of a well-conducted, tightly fought swerve

Brooklands track as it was before the Campbell road circuit was added in the Paddock area. Racing was run anti-clockwise and one lap of the Outer Circuit measured 2.8 miles. Norton BS and BRS machines were timed over the one kilometre stretch on the Railway Straight.

through the Fork, or enjoy the excitement of a swoop off the lip of the Home Banking into the Railway Straight.

Brain-child of a far-seeing motoring sportsman, H. F. Locke-King, Brooklands was built to the design of Col H. C. L. Holden near Weybridge, Surrey, as a 2.8-mile kidney-shaped circuit with a sharp, steeply banked turn at one end and a widely radiused, more gently graded sweep at the other— the Home and the Byfleet Bankings respectively.

These were connected on the north by the Railway Straight, running alongside the main London-to-Portsmouth line, and on the southern side by a short, inwardly curving stretch that forked midway, the left leg forming the Finishing Straight, which rejoined the main loop beyond the Home Banking.

The track provided three main courses: first, the Full Course, which was right round the outer circuit, the actual distance measured on the 50-foot line from the inner perimeter being 2.767 miles per lap; secondly, the Short or Double Twelve Course which used the Finishing Straight to cut out the Home Banking, giving a distance of 2.616 miles

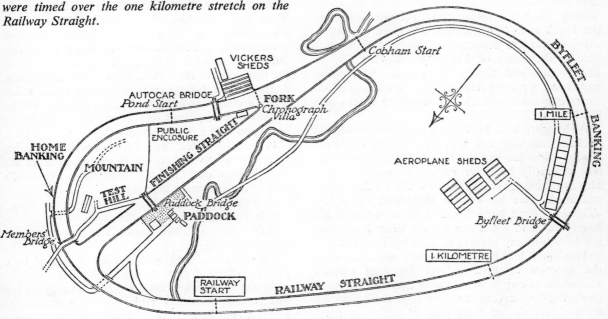

per lap; and lastly, the Mountain Course which used only the Home Banking and the Finishing Straight to give a distance of 1.17 miles. Later a simulated road course, the Campbell Circuit, was introduced.

The circuit was used anti-clockwise, and the principal motorcycle start line was at the Fork where the Finishing Straight broke away from the full course. Here, facing the sheds of the Vickers aeroplane works, was the timekeepers' hut, always known as Chronograph Villa.

On the east of the Finishing Straight was the Test Hill with gradients rising to a maximum of 1 in 4. On the west lay the Paddock, the club-house of the Brooklands Automobile Racing Club, and the numerous workshops, huts and sheds rented by the trade and by the tuning fraternity, a pioneer among whom was, of course, the legendary Dan O'Donovan.

Although, earlier, there had been at least one private match between pairs of riders, the first full-scale motorcycle race was held on Easter Monday 1908 with 24 entrants on machines of all sizes up to a couple of prodigious V-twins of 1,000 cc. The first prize was a choice between a purse of 20 sovereigns or a cup and, as little was known about their personal or mechanical capabilities, all starters set off from scratch. It was a two-lap race and the winner, W. E. Cook, on an NLG Peugeot twin, averaged 63 mph.

From that beginning sprang an immense wave of enthusiasm for Brooklands track racing. In the next year the still flourishing British Motor Cycle Racing Club ('Bemsee') was formed, adopting the Track as its headquarters. The need for handi-capping quickly became obvious and those two oldest inhabitants of Chronograph Villa, A. V. Ebblewhite and George Reynolds, a bassoon maker and a printer respectively, were launched on their long careers of closely watching clocks and form.

Although it also provided an aerodrome for the Vickers company and a flying club (as well as a sewage farm for the local authority), Brooklands was primarily built for racing. However, it was also available for record attacks. On 'off days' any-one could take his vehicle there and for a few shillings bounce himself round the concrete to his heart's content. I did this myself when I received my 15th birthday present of a 2¼ hp Royal Ruby.

The Track had barely come into existence when the practice of making and breaking records started on its way to what was to become compara-tively big business. In the early days there were all sorts of records and many ways of achieving them.

Often they were set up during the course of races, or the circuit would be cleared after an event for a record session. Alternatively, an individual or a company would hire the track and the services of the officials for a special attack.

Very early in the game the FICM took control of world records, sorted out the classes, and laid down stringent regulations for the conduct and requirements of 'attempts at records'. Today the official register of motorcycle world records is a vast tome in which the derring deeds of many mighty men are clinically detailed in terms of time, distance and speed. These are the successes; un-recordable are the vastly more numerous 'boss-shots', devastating failures and heartbreaking near-misses.

It would be impossible here to try to do more than outline the story of Norton involvement with Brooklands in racing and records. On the racing side the marque, both solo and sidecar, was ridden to victories by hundreds of men during the track's 30 years of life. To name only a handful would be unfair to many more. But how about the ladies? More than a few brave girls donned leathers and helmets and battled it out with the men, and three particularly merit a place in this Norton story for they were all recipients of a unique and irreplace-able distinction—a Brooklands Gold Star.

The Star—a piece of yellow metal about the size of a shirt button—was awarded to all Bemsee members who at one of the Club's meetings, lapped the Outer Circuit at 100 mph or more. First to win one was Herbert le Vack in 1922. Some 200 Stars were awarded, and in 1934 Miss Florence Blenkiron, on a 500 cc model, became the first woman recipient. In the same season Miss Beatrice Shilling, also on a 500, topped 'the ton'. Then in the final year of the Track, Miss Theresa Wallach, a determined little person who had twice made unaccompanied solo motorcycle crossings of the Sahara desert, gained one of the last Stars to be presented—on a 350 machine!

Francis Beart tells how Theresa walked into his track workshop and asked if she could have his 348 International for the following week-end's BMCRC Clubman's meeting.

'It'll cost you a fiver,' said Beart.

'I haven't got one,' was the reply.

'Try some of the bonus barons,' suggested Francis.

Soon she was back with the £5—provided by a publicity-minded chocolate manufacturer.

At the rain-soaked meeting Theresa's flying lap was turned at 101.64 mph—to the considerable surprise of Beart's then head jockey, Johnny

Lockett, who had never been able to make that 350 go into a three-figure lap! After the war Miss Wallach emigrated to Chicago where she successfully set up her own Norton dealership and tuning establishment.

Any account of Nortons' part in the world of motorcycle speed records must inevitably start with O'Donovan, for the wonderful BS machines came from his Brooklands workshop. He not only rode the mounts he prepared but he launched on their way to fame such celebrated record breakers as Rex Judd, Bert Denly, Nigel Spring and Chris Staniland.

As far back as 1915 O'Donovan had covered the flying kilometre at 82.85 mph on a 490 cc single-cylinder side-valve Norton with direct belt drive. Judd, when he joined O'Donovan's outfit in 1920, upped this speed to 85 mph on a similar machine and a year later, still with a side-valver but now fitted with a gearbox and all-chain drive, Rex became the first rider to exceed 90 mph on a 500 cc machine.

When the ohv Norton appeared in 1922 Judd, as told in Chapter 5, succeeded in setting the flying kilometre world record at 89.92 mph and a little later he reached 98.50 mph on a one-way run.

Attacks on the sprint-type kilometre and mile records were conducted with almost ferocious rivalry, one man after another clipping away a few split seconds. But it became increasingly apparent to the public that a short, spectacular burst of all-out speed revealed practically nothing about a machine's powers of endurance. Attention therefore turned more towards the long-distance records. Of these there were many, ranging up to the Double 12 Hours, and the one that offered the greatest prize in terms of publicity was the 'One-Hour'. This had been established first at the Canning Town Track, when in 1907 Charlie Collier covered 51.3 miles in 60 minutes on a 432 Matchless JAP.

The Norton name first appeared in the Hour list in 1920 when, during the course of a Brooklands race, Victor Horsman averaged 71.68 mph on a single-speeder. During the 1920s Horsman broke the Hour record on eight occasions.

In the 1923/4 season the Norton-O'Donovan team sent former butcher's boy Albert Denly into the fray and he raised the 500 cc Hour figure four times, eventually reaching 87.07 mph. Then followed a period when big multi-cylinder mounts predominated.

In January 1927 Nigel Spring replaced O'Donovan as Nortons' track supremo and his aim was the all-important first 100 miles in the Hour on a 500 cc machine. The mount prepared for this job was a 490 cc ohv Norton and Bert Denly was appointed to its saddle. A 588 cc counterpart was also got ready. Preliminary attempts produced a 96.67 mph average for 100 kilometres with the smaller machine and a flying kilo record of 109.22 for the 600 cc machine. In June, on the 490 model at the Montlhéry circuit, Denly rode the Hour at 95.02 mph. After a couple of days' interval devoted to further tuning he went out again and on June 28 1927 covered 100.58 miles in the 60 minutes—perhaps one of the most remarkable successes in motorcycle speed history, for the machine was constructed from standard components and had no wind-cheating fitments whatsoever.

On these laurels Norton rested for four years until Bill Lacey took a 490 cc overhead cam-shaft machine to Montlhéry and, on September 29 1931, sent the '500 Hour' up to 110.80 mph. This figure stood for a further four years until Jimmy Guthrie went to the same circuit with a works-prepared, alcohol-propelled 'Joe Motor', and on October 18 1935 upped the 60 minutes spell to 114.09 mph.

Eighteen years were to pass before Nortons made their next—and last—attack on the record, which in the meantime had gone to Piero Taruffi who had had two successful bouts (1937 and 1939) with fully enclosed four-cylinder super-charged 500 cc Gileras. On November 9 1953 Ray Amm took his Kneeler around Montlhéry for an hour's circuitry at an average of 133.71 mph—over 6 mph up on Taruffi's best and on an unblown, single-cylinder motor running on petrol at that!

Only twice since has the Hour record been raised—on each occasion by a streamlined four, the riders being Bob McIntyre (Gilera, Monza, 1957, 141.37 mph) and Mike Hailwood (MV, Daytona, 1964, 144.83 mph). Bob rode a 350!

It looks as though there is a '1½-ton' prize awaiting somebody at some time in the not-too-distant future.

Chapter 24

The Featherbed Years (Part 1)

THE TWELVE YEARS from 1950 to 1961 saw the fortunes of Norton Motors fluctuating with the unpredictability of a British barometer. During this period racing activities varied from stunning successes to the end of the production of Manx machines. There were exciting models added to the roadster ranges, and old favourites disappeared. Many new names, both in the sport and in the factory, became associated with the marque and, in the midst of the era, ownership of the company changed hands.

So much occurred in Norton history during these 12 critical years that some form of compression is essential, even if only the major happenings are to be contained within the covers of this book. What follows is therefore a year-by-year record of the salient incidents that affected the firm's progress, which will assist readers interested in pin-pointing the oft-recurring changes in design that were made in this period. Blow-by-blow accounts of the vast number of races and other events in which Nortons figured are out of the question; never before in the story of motorcycle sport was there such a surge of enthusiasm among the fans as that which came in with the 1950s.

1950

During 1950 long-standing race and lap records were broken in almost every major event. Increases in speed largely stemmed from improved fuel, the octane rating of which had been raised to 80 as against 75 in the previous years. Better handling also contributed, especially so in the case of Nortons, which had the benefit of an entirely new design of pivoted rear fork, duplex loop frame. Compared with the old plunger-sprung 'garden gate', this gave such a vastly more comfortable ride that it was promptly nicknamed the 'Featherbed'.

A frame of this type had appeared earlier at an England versus Ireland moto-cross match staged at Brands Hatch, and had been constructed with the help of Artie Bell in the Belfast workshop of the McCandless brothers, Rex and Cromie. A modified version was adopted and patented by Norton and, fitted with Roadholder

front forks, was ready so early in the season that Geoff Duke was able to give it an airing in April when winning the ACU's International Road Race Meeting held on the Blandford circuit, in Dorset.

In the main the 'Joe Motors', both 350 and 500, used to power the new machines were not very much different from the double ohc types of 1949, but on the better fuel the 500 could run up to 7,000 rpm. The crankcase and flywheel assembly had been stiffened and the cylinder head re-cast as an all-aluminium unit with nickel-iron inserted valve seats. This arrangement replaced the bronze 'skull' pattern. It also had the upper camshaft bevel housing cast integrally with the fins surrounding it, whilst the hairpin valve springs were left exposed.

It is, of course, a matter of legend that these first Featherbeds made their TT debut a double hat-trick, with all four of the works riders—Bell, Daniell, Duke and Lockett—beating George Meier's 1939 Senior race record.

The finishing orders were: *Junior*—1, Bell; 2, Duke; 3, Daniell; 6, Lockett. *Senior*—1, Duke; 2, Bell; 3, Lockett; 5, Daniell. Duke's Senior winning speed was 92.27 mph and his fastest lap in 24 minutes 16 seconds, 93.33 mph, broke Daniell's 12-year-old '91' record by nearly 2.5 mph.

Nortons won the Manufacturers' team prize in both races and Duke, R. H. Dale and W. H. C. McCandless were the British Motor Cycle Racing Club's Norton team that took the Club prize.

The next event on the international calendar was the Belgian GP, run on the much-modified and faster Spa circuit. It was here that a quite unexpected hazard made its appearance—tyre trouble. In the 500 cc event, first Johnny Lockett and then Geoff Duke were eliminated from positions at the front of a field that included Gilera and MV fours by large lumps of rubber parting from the canvas of their rear tyres. Duke was, in fact, about to win the race when this happened to him.

Earlier in the event one of the worst crashes in motorcycle racing had occurred when a group of leading riders tangled and spilled across the track; Les Graham and Artie Bell were hurled under a stilt-legged broadcasting box situated on the track's edge. Miraculously Les was able to walk away no more than shaken, but Artie's injuries were so grave that only highly skilled medical attention plus his own superb physique enabled him to survive, though he was never able to race a motorcycle again.

Hurriedly the tyre makers produced a new 'mix' in time for the Dutch TT, but in this event not only the entire Norton team, which now included Dickie Dale, but also that of AJS retired with broken treads.

For the Ulster GP Norton changed the make of tyre and the specification from 3 in front, 3.25 in rear on 19 in rims to 3 in × 21 in front and 3.5 in × 20 in rear. This move evidently had the desired effect for Duke won the race at nearly 100 mph, with the fastest lap at 101.77 mph. He went on to secure a 350/500 cc double in the Italian GP, handsomely beating the Gileras of Masetti and Bandirola and the MVs of Artesiani and Milani.

In the Manx Grand Prix Peter Romaine, using Francis Beart Nortons, gained a win in the Senior race, after having been second in the Junior to Don Crossley whose AJS was fitted with an oversize tank that enabled the rider to cover the six laps non-stop.

1951

There was no Earls Court Show in 1950. Had there been, Norton would have exhibited a little altered 1951 range of roadster models. The singles had bigger, better looking oil tanks; the side-valvers had steady struts between front down tube and cylinder head; and there was a more generous application of chromium plate on front forks, brake plates and small fittings. The firm could also have displayed the 500 cc World Road Racing Manufacturers' Championship award, as well as a repeat showing of Eric Oliver's Sidecar Championship certificate.

In August the double-knocker Featherbed-framed Manx Models 30 and 40 were listed for the first time as production racers. The general specification which covered these two machines, later to be classified as the longstroke models, is given below.

Apart from engine capacity and gear ratios, the 30M 500 was practically identical to its 40M 350 counterpart. The respective differences were:

Model 30: Bore 79.62 mm, stroke 100 mm, 499 cc. Ratios, with 23T engine sprocket—4.64,

5.1, 6.18, 8.22 : 1.

Model 40: Bore 71 mm, stroke 88 mm, 348 cc. Ratios, with 18T engine sprocket—5.6, 5.67, 6.85, 9.12 : 1.

Both models had twin overhead camshaft valve gear; head and barrel were in light alloy; the piston was of forged light alloy and the con-rod a forged H-section steel component with a double-row roller bearing big-end; the crankcase was of magnesium alloy; and a Lucas racing magneto and an Amal RN-type carburettor were fitted.

The Norton four-speed gearbox had remotely controlled positive-stop foot operation and the three-plate clutch used Ferodo inserts. All joints of the duplex loop swinging fork frame were bronze-welded and Roadholder front forks were fitted. The magnesium alloy brakes were 8 in diameter front and 7 in diameter rear and the alloy rims carried 3 in × 19 in ribbed and 3.50 in × 19 in studded tyres.

Light alloy was used for the rubber-mounted racing mudguards and the fuel (5½ gallons) and oil (1 gallon) tanks. The petrol tank was quickly detachable, being secured by a central strap. A cambox-driven 8,000 rpm indicator was included in the standard specification. Extras were a wire gauze fly screen, racing number plates and megaphone exhaust.

The works racing team for the 1951 season was cast as Geoff Duke, Johnny Lockett and Dickie Dale, but just before the TT meeting Dale was struck down by illness and the choice of a replacement lay between two hard-riding Norton men, Harry Hinton from Australia and Yorkshire's Jack Brett. The decision went to Brett and he amply repaid it, riding loyally on the Bracebridge Street marque in many tough battles—until he retired in 1961.

Except for experiments with reversed cone megaphones, hardly any changes were made to the previous year's racing mounts and Duke, Lockett and Brett, in that order, rang up another Norton hat-trick in the Junior event.

The feat was nearly repeated in the Senior. Geoff Duke led from start to finish and pushed the lap record up to 95.22 mph, but his team mates both fell from high places, Lockett with a broken chain on the last lap and Brett through a spill when he was lying second. These retirements let Bill Doran (AJS) into second berth, but the remaining places on the leader board were filled by the Nortons of Cromie McCandless, Tommy McEwan, Manliff Barrington, A. L. Parry and

Eric Briggs. Last of the 21 bronze replica winners (only the first six gained silver replicas) was a newcomer from Southern Rhodesia, W. R. Amm (Norton).

The Continental *Grandes Epreuves* saw ups and downs for Bracebridge Street. Nevertheless, Duke achieved double Junior/Senior victories in the Belgian and Ulster GPs, a 350 success in the Italian GP and a 500 win in the Dutch TT. And he ended the season World Champion in both classes. Norton Motors were the Manufacturers' Champions in 350, 500 and Sidecar categories, Eric Oliver again being the individual champion of the charioteers.

Among the year's batch of promising new boys from the Commonwealth, K. T. Kavanagh was outstanding and his efforts were rewarded when Joe Craig made him a fourth member of the works team for the Ulster Grand Prix.

No alterations were made to the standard production machines for the next season, but just before the Show it was announced that, for the time being and for export only, there was to be a de luxe version of the Dominator, designated the Model 88 and employing the swinging rear fork Featherbed frame. This news caused no great surprise, for the Norton team in that September's International Six Days Trial had ridden machines so constructed. Finished in polychromatic grey, the 88 was much admired at the Show for its good looks. It weighed 380 lb, as against the 413 lb of the plunger-sprung Model 7.

1952

The oft-repeated question: 'Will Nortons produce a multi to match the Italian fire engines?' got its answer when, in the spring of 1952, details of the new season's Bracebridge Street raceware were released. Joe Craig was continuing to rely on the single-cylinder 'thumpers' but some intricate slide-rule work had resulted in yet another variation on the bore and stroke theme. In search of higher rpm without increased piston speed he had virtually squared the 499 cc dimensions to 85.93 mm × 86 mm; this was said to enable the use of larger valves. The Junior model measurements were 75.9 mm × 77 mm, giving 348.3 cc.

For some time technicians had wondered why Nortons had not copied the Velocette practice of completely surrounding the camshaft vertical drive with finning. Joe had done half the job in 1950 when he produced all-round finning on the cylinder head. Now he also applied it to the barrel, and even the lower bevel bearing housing was finned. The then new type of Lucas rotating magnet

magneto was adopted and a modified venturi on the GP Amal carburettor was used to control air eddies around the intake.

The Featherbed frame employed more welding, though Sif-bronzing was still used for the seat sub-assembly. Sintered bronze bushes replaced the Silentbloc bonded-rubber units in the rear fork pivot and heavier, forward-leaning rear suspension legs were fitted. An immediately noticeable change was the transfer of the rear brake to the offside of the machine. Not only was heat from the drum thus kept away from the aluminium sprocket but also the secondary chain could be more liberally oiled without risk of lubricant reaching the brake-shoes. The two-leading-shoe type of brake was retained for the front wheel. Application of the offside rear brake by the nearside pedal was by a Bowdenex flexible cable.

For the TT the Senior Nortons were equipped with 3 in × 18 in front and 4 in × 16 in rear tyres. For some of the Continental races a 3.50 in × 18 in cover was used at the rear. Norton sidecar drivers were provided with 3.50 in × 16 in flat-treaded tyres.

The factory foursome consisted of Geoff Duke, Ken Kavanagh, Dubliner H. R. Armstrong (who, after a Manx GP initiation, had ridden well on TT AJS and Velocette machines from 1949 to 1951), and D. E. Bennett, due to make a June debut after a Senior Norton first place with race and lap records in the previous year's Manx GP. An employee at Bracebridge Street, Dave Bennett, a most promising young rider with a style reminiscent of Tim Hunt's, was destined never to achieve his great ambition of a TT works ride. A month before he crashed fatally while riding in the Swiss GP at Berne, his first international road race.

To re-form his TT quartet Wizard Craig waved his wand at Lancashire lad A. L. Parry, who was entered on a couple of notably fast Nortons already ridden with distinction by John Storr. They belonged to the chief of Elms Metals Ltd, Ernie Earles, whose ingenious leading link front fork was about to be widely adopted, notably on Les Graham's MV 4 and later as a standard production fitting by BMW.

Nortons' chances of a team prize in the Junior looked to be well nigh shock-proof. Nominated the No 1 team were Duke, Kavanagh and Reg Armstrong; No 2 consisted of Len Parry, Ray Amm and Cromie McCandless, the last-named riding the smaller of a brace of Beart models. But the plan went amiss, Kavanagh and Parry both had last-lap retirements, while Amm crashed at Braddan Bridge on the fifth lap.

Duke led throughout and, after a stern tussle with New Zealand's Rod Coleman (AJS), Armstrong held second place. Geoff's 90.29 mph average was a course record but he just failed to better his previous year's lap record.

In the Senior Duke kept ahead of Graham's MV until a faulty clutch put him out after four laps. The chase was then taken up by Armstrong who moved to the front on the sixth lap and crossed the line a winner—with a broken primary chain; Amm was third to Graham, and McCandless's 496 cc Beart-Norton was sixth. No records were broken, Duke's fastest lap being set at 94.88 mph.

The end-of-season World Championship tables recorded the overwhelming supremacy of the 350 Nortons, which won seven out of the eight classic races, Duke leading the riders' section with four first places. In the 500 cc class Norton had to take second place to Gilera whose Umberto Masetti did most of the work.

1953

This year saw the end of the plunger-sprung frame, all models previously so equipped being converted to swinging fork rear suspension. The Big Four, 16H, 18 and 500T retained their rigid frames. The ES2 and Model 7 Dominator had their rear ends adapted to take the pivot fork and the two Internationals were given Featherbed frames.

The 'springers' had a new design of silencer, and rockerbox lubrication for Dominator engines was improved. Slight changes to the Trials model reduced weight.

In February the startling news of a proposed (and subsequently consolidated) merger between Norton Motors Ltd and Associated Motor Cycles Ltd was announced. Gilbert Smith told reporters that the Norton directors had received an offer from AMC (which then included the AJS, Matchless, James and Francis-Barnett marques) to acquire the entire share capital, and the Norton directors, agreeing to sell their holdings amounting to some 50 per cent, were recommending other shareholders to do likewise. Gilbert Smith added that he expected his company would continue as a separate entity and that the same keen rivalry in sporting competition would continue.

To back up the latter part of that prediction Joe Craig went ahead with preparations for the racing season. Before the end of February Ken Kavanagh was seen circling the Montlhéry track on an extraordinary-looking streamliner that was to become renowned as the Norton Kneeler, since the rider flattened his body on a mattress on low-slung top tubes, rested his shins in a pair of troughs, and arranged his feet alongside the rear spring units. Pannier fuel tanks were arranged each side of the engine and nose and tail were semi-enclosed by fairings. A bystander, watching Kennie Kavanagh endeavouring to worm his way aboard this strange,

No motorcycles were more popular in their time with sporting riders than the International Nortons—fast road machines capable of excellent racing performance. This picture shows the last of the plunger-sprung frame type; after 1952, Featherbed frames were adopted.

fish-like contraption, was heard to remark: 'This Norton really is unapproachable!'

Leaving the 350 cc engine dimensions unchanged, Craig turned to an even shorter stroke for the bigger banger. In order to take advantage of a lighter connecting rod he adopted bore and stroke measurements of 88 mm × 82 mm, giving 498.7 cc capacity.

Modifications to both Junior and Senior machines included a system of oil cooling for exhaust valves, a stronger clutch, with the shock absorber back on the engine shaft, and a totally revised system of carburation that used an over-spill weir float chamber, surplus fuel being returned to the tank by a small pump driven from the inlet camshaft. When Ray Amm rode the 350 cc Streamliner in the North West 200 race, the pump was used to lift fuel from the pannier tanks.

The official team for the TT was Amm, Brett and Kavanagh; Duke, Armstrong and Dale had transferred to Gilera. Syd Lawton was invited to make a Norton works quartet but this excellent rider from Southampton was hospitalised after a crash during practice and Joe had to make another choice. John Storr was away on the Continent and could not reach the Island in time to qualify, so the 'Professor' made a remarkably prescient decision; he offered the fourth-man position to a 19-year-old lad who was that year making his first acquaintance with the Mountain Circuit — John Surtees. But again an injury during practice (on a Lightweight machine) intervened, and poor John had to forego the chance of a TT debut on a works banger — through nothing more serious than a sprained wrist.

Amm practised on the Kneeler but both the 350 and 500 cc versions were withdrawn from the races. An experimental leading-link front fork was tried and abandoned, as also were the small wheels, a return being made to 19 in diameter rims. Petrol tanks were narrowed at the rear to allow riders to tuck their knees in more closely.

In the Junior race Ray Amm led all the way to finish in record time, beating team mate Kavanagh by 9⅗ seconds. Both men broke the lap record, Ray's faster speed being 91.82 mph. With Brett taking fourth place, the trio bagged the Manufacturers' team award for Norton.

Just one lap of the Senior had been ridden when Les Graham's tragic death came with a crash at the foot of Bray Hill. The popular MV rider was lying second to Geoff Duke, who was himself robbed of the lead by a fifth-lap tumble at Quarter Bridge. At the same time Kavanagh lost a chain, the same fate that had put him out of the previous

year's Senior. That left Ray Amm and Jack Brett in final 1-2 positions, Brett having overhauled Armstrong's Gilera on the last lap. Amm repeated his Monday's success by breaking both course and lap records. His third and fastest lap in 23 minutes 15 seconds, 97.41 mph, raised Duke's 1952 record by nearly 3 mph. At this rate of speed increase it looked as though 1954 might see the achievement of the magic 'ton'.

R. D. Keeler won the Senior Clubman's TT on one of the new Featherbed Internationals and a new award, the *Motor Cycling* Trophy for the best agent-entered rider, went to P. A. Davey, one of the scores of protégés of Reg Dearden, whose enthusiastic support of both the TT and the Manx GP helped so many men to success on the machines he provided and prepared right up until his death in 1972.

Italian and German machines dominated the World Championship classic solo races except in the Ulster Grand Prix where New Zealander Ken Mudford and Australian Ken Kavanagh respectively gained 350 and 500 cc victories. The three-wheeler category gave yet another drivers' title (the fourth in five years) to Eric Oliver whose four race wins also gained the Manufacturers' award for Norton.

Just before the Show Oliver and Ray Amm indulged in two days of record breaking at Montlhéry with 350 and 500 cc engines in the Streamliner frame. Lapping at speeds close on 145 mph, Amm included in their bag of 61 new records the One Hour world record at 133.71 mph.

The Streamliner was a big attraction on the Norton stand at the Earls Court Show.

1954

This was a salient—and a sorrowful—year for it was the last in which the two British racing companies, Norton and AJS, gave full works support with special machines to the World Championships.

The 'Joe Motors', the AJS Porcupines and triple-knocker 7Rs were making their last official appearances on the speed circuits. AMC's head men at Woolwich—and it went for Bracebridge Street, too—were finding the cost of full-scale factory racing disproportionately high. However, it was not until near the end of 1954 that the Plumstead boardroom began to get the jitters, so Craig and his henchmen blithely went into the new season to see what could be done to extract even greater performance from a single-cylinder, air-cooled, four-stroke, naturally aspirated machine running on straight petrol.

The new Norton racers differed from their predecessors in two main respects. One, obvious at a glance, was the use of an outside flywheel. The other was that both the 500 and 350 engines had ultra-short strokes, being 90 mm × 78.4 mm and 78 mm × 73 mm respectively.

The transfer of the flywheel effect to the outside of the engine provided room in the crankcase for an entirely re-designed and very much stiffer crank assembly, supported by heavy duty two-row roller bearings on the drive side. Engine breathing was through a flap valve device on the front of the crankcase. 'Upstairs' there were new cams and the carburettor float chamber was not scavenged. There were certain modifications to the frames, chiefly aimed, especially with the Junior model, at lighter weight. The rear brake was controlled via a cross-over rod running through the fork pivot and the front brake was equipped with a kind of extractor fan in the hub, intended to lower pressure in the drum and induce an increased flow of air. A five-speed gearbox was available for use on circuits that particularly required an extra ratio. On occasions the machines were raced 'naked'; for the TT Amm's was fitted with a peculiarly shaped frontal fairing that projected so far forward that it was dubbed 'the Proboscis'. Brett's machine had the same nose-piece without side fairing.

Nortons had two teams in both the Junior and Senior TTs. No 1 comprised Ray Amm, Jack Brett and Bob Keeler, and No 2 was a Commonwealth trio—Australians Gordon Laing and Maurice Quincey and South African Rudy Allison.

In the Junior the first Norton home was Keeler's in third place behind the Ajays of Rod Coleman and Derek Farrant. Amm went out after four laps having raised the record to 94.61 mph. Brett got no further than Ramsey.

Bad weather delayed the start of the Senior race by 1½ hours, and then, as conditions got worse, the stewards ended the event after four laps had been completed. At that stage Amm had taken the lead from Duke (Gilera) after Geoff had stopped to refuel at the end of his third lap. The winning speed, 88.12 mph, was nearly 6 mph down on the previous year's record.

The works team won the Manufacturers' prize and Amm, Brett and Keeler also won the Club award.

This year saw the re-introduction (after nearly 30 years) of the Sidecar TT, run over the new 10.8-mile Clypse circuit. Against strong competition from Continental BMW drivers Eric Oliver drove his Norton-Watsonian outfit round the ten laps at 68.87 mph; his fastest lap was made at 70.85 mph. The Manufacturers' prize went to Watsonian Sidecars Ltd—F. Taylor, L. W. Taylor and Frenchman Jacques Drion, all Norton-powered, as were the Club team winners, W. G. Boddice, J. Beeton and F. Taylor.

It was largely through the enthusiasm of Eric Oliver and Watsonian chief R. G. J. Watson that the sidecar event came about and it was fitting that their efforts should be so signally rewarded. Throughout the story of sidecar racing in this period, no man did more to further this exciting form of sport than Ronnie Watson, whose factory produced many magnificent outfits.

An arm injury in a minor race robbed Oliver of the chance of the World Sidecar Championship title which he had held with one interruption since 1949. For the first time since its inception, the World Championship saw the five category winners all driving foreign machines.

The Norton road machine range offered in 1954 had no special innovations but it lacked the mount that might have been a commercial winner. This was the ohv high-camshaft 250 (66 mm × 72.6 mm) which developed 13.5 bhp at 6,500 rpm. The sloping cylinder unit-construction engine was carried in a modified Featherbed frame. It never went into production but the prototype, which was extensively tested, can be inspected in the National Motor Museum at Beaulieu, Hants.

Nineteen-fifty-four saw the Manx production racers carrying the short stroke motors of square dimensions—76 mm × 76.7 mm, 348 cc, and 86 mm × 85.62 mm, 499 cc—with 'squish' heads. Changes were made to big-end eyes, valves, springs and other items that practically ruled out any interchangeability of parts with the earlier long stroke types. Two-leading-shoe front brakes were fitted.

Chapter 25

The Featherbed Years (Part 2)

1955

AFTER an unbroken run of over 45 years there were no side-valve-engined machines in the Norton range. The Big Four, which had first appeared at the Stanley Show in 1907, and its smaller brother the 16H, as well as the latter's ohv counterpart, the Model 18, were all abandoned, along with the 500T Trials mount.

Mainly to meet the needs of customers requiring a sturdy sidecar puller, the 596 cc ohv model 19 was resuscitated and revitalised, and was offered with either a rigid or a spring frame.

The whole range now had light-alloy cylinder heads and a wealth of chromium plate, especially on the Dominator 88, which also had full-width alloy hubs. The Manx racers had a flanged timing-side main bearing.

In February came a pronouncement from Bracebridge Street and Plumstead concerning future racing policy. The Norton and AMC statements were aligned and confirmed the rumours that had been circulating since the 1954 show. A quote from Gilbert Smith's statement

General arrangement of the F-type unit construction, outside flywheel horizontal (Guzzi Gambalungha style) engine that would, but for a change in Norton racing policy, have driven the factory team machines in 1955.

sums up the situation: 'Feeling that further progress with the development of special "works" machines will lead to the demise of private-owner racing, the company has decided to revert to its original policy of racing a type of machine which can be sold to private owners'.

There was to be no support for the World Championship series but certain selected major races, such as the TT and Ulster GP, which assisted development, would be contested. Machines would be raced 'naked' as streamlining 'from the private owner's point of view was undesirable . . . and could be dangerous'.

For Nortons' team two 21-year-old riders had already been nominated, London's John Surtees and Derbyshire's John Hartle. The third member was expected to be Ray Amm, but he had already opted out. He had transferred to MV, and was fated to crash mortally at the season-opening Imola meeting in Italy in April. Jack Brett joined Surtees and Hartle and on the eve of TT practising details were published of the modifications that had been made to the standard Manx models to turn them into 'prototype production racers'.

The dohc engines had new cams, improved shapes for ports and valves and the isolated weir-type carburettor and the rotating magnet magneto were used. Frame alterations included

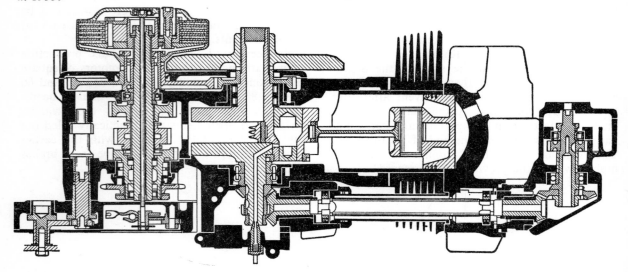

larger outside front fork springs; smaller, stay-less front mudguards; welded-on handlebar controls (no air lever); and a stiffened rearguard with a better seat. The bronze-bushed rear suspension system was 'pinched' from the earlier works machines, as were a number of minor details such as spring-controlled clutch and brake lever adjusters.

Although the factory had turned its back on any kind of streamlining, some private owners were thinking otherwise. One of the most interesting adventures in this field was seen in the full enclosure of the Nortons prepared for the already up-and-coming Glasgow rider Bob McIntyre by fellow citizen and highly skilful tuner-sponsor Joe Potts, whose stable also included Alastair King.

In the Junior TT Bob Mac handled his 'dustbin' brilliantly, sandwiching himself between two other enclosed machines, the Guzzis of W. A. Lomas and Cecil Sandford. The naked Nortons of John Surtees, Maurice Quincey (also on a factory machine) and John Hartle completed the leader board, but an early spill by Jack Brett in Ramsey robbed Norton of the team prize, which was not awarded.

Brett made up for his lapse when he finished fourth in the Senior race on the first British machine home. Next was McIntyre (unstreamlined) and, as Hartle and Surtees were both finishers, Norton gained the Manufacturers' team prize.

Geoff Duke's winning speed on the Gilera 4 was 97.93 mph and his fastest circuit in 22 minutes 39 seconds was initially announced as the first TT 'ton' lap, but it was later corrected to 99.97 mph!

Having stood down in the World Championships the Norton team waited for the Ulster GP, but in the meantime John Surtees scored success after success on the British short circuits.

At the Dundrod circuit in Ireland John Hartle really showed what a production racer could do. In the 350 cc Ulster GP he was beaten by only 24 seconds and in the 500 cc event by as close a margin as 6 seconds, his victor in both events being Bill Lomas on Guzzi streamliners. Surtees, who finished third in the 350 class, subsequently announced his intention to transfer to the MV team for the next season.

On August 30 Charles Anthony Vandervell, former Norton chairman and father of Tony Vandervell (of Vanwall car fame), died at the age of 89. Up to the merger with AMC he had been Norton Motors' largest individual shareholder. His last public engagement had been in 1949 when, at a Savoy Hotel luncheon to celebrate Nortons' hat-trick at Daytona, he presented Francis Beart with an International model.

At the end of the year Joe Craig resigned to settle in semi-retirement in Holland.

1956

In accordance with the new policy, the 'over-the-counter' 30M and 40M models for 1956 were virtually identical to the machines raced by Surtees, Brett and Hartle in the previous year.

The ohv roadsters were compacted into a five-model range. Out, after eight years of useful work, went the Model 7 Dominator, being replaced by a 597 cc version of the Model 88. This Model 99 was specially made to take advantage of the premium grade fuels that had recently become available in the home and export fields. Its cylinder dimensions were 68 mm bore × 82 mm stroke, with a compression ratio of 7.4:1. Wire-bound pistons were used.

Not since pre-war days had there been a 350 cc ohv machine in the catalogue. Now the Model 50 appeared, which was virtually a 348 cc replica of the ES2 with 71 mm × 88 mm measurements. The ohc 350 and 500 cc Internationals were still listed but henceforth they were built only to special order.

Midway through the year gearboxes made by AMC at Plumstead, but with Bracebridge Street clutches, were adopted.

A month or so before the TT Herbert Hopwood returned after a seven-year spell with BSA to join the Norton board with responsibility for design and production.

Alan Wilson, who had been on the sales and service side of the business, became competitions manager. A new director, G. Alec Skinner, was appointed in May and shortly after, when Leslie Hepburn, who had been sales manager for many years, resigned, W. J. 'Bill' Smith came from Norton dealers Rossleigh of Edinburgh to succeed him.

By the end of 1955 the 350 and 500 cc TT models had been producing just over 40 and 50 bhp respectively. A considerable improvement on these maxima was obtained in 1956 by cylinder head and piston modifications which further improved the 'squish' effect. This, plus the availability of 100 octane fuel, allowed compression ratios to be raised to about 10.5:1. The inlet as well as the exhaust valve was sodium-cooled and a modified cam gave a reduced seating velocity, allowing higher 'safe' engine revolutions. Slightly larger chokes were also used.

Stiffer brake drums with increased cooling fin areas, a reduced frontal area through shorter forks, and shorter and stiffer rear frames were further changes. Throughout the season no engine failures were experienced.

John Surtees having 'gone foreign' to MV, Norton had yet again to scan the available talent for a team mate for Brett and Hartle. The selection went to a husky scrambling/trialsman from Welling in Kent, Alan Trow, whose only experience of the Island course was in a couple of Manx GP races.

The result of this choice was that the Bracebridge Street trio won the Senior Manufacturers' team award; Trow finished sixth in the Junior and seventh in the Senior. In the latter race John Hartle and Jack Brett were second and third. Hartle (who had finished third in the Junior) was only some 90 seconds behind the Senior winner, Surtees, and by virtue of a fine win in the 500 cc Ulster GP he came third in the World Championship table, having contested only two of the six classic events!

Bob McIntyre, who had been offered a season with Gilera and had elected to stay aboard the Nortons of his sponsor Joe Potts, had a bag of successes during the year and among the many Norton-powered sidecars that of P. V. 'Pip' Harris was hard to beat. In the Manx GP another Potts protégé, Jimmy Buchan, scored a double and Nortons were first, second and third in both races.

1957

On March 7 1957, while motoring near Innsbruck, Austria, Joe Craig, MIMechE, MSAE, had a heart attack and was killed when his car went out of control. Aged 59, the 'Wizard of Waft', as Graham Walker had named him, had, but for a wartime spell at Woolwich, been with Nortons since he gave up racing in 1928 until his retirement barely a year before his death. And there is no need for me to emphasise the enormous influence this quiet-spoken, deep-thinking Ulsterman had on racing motorcycle development. The fantastic results he obtained from his triple role of team-manager, tactician and technician are never likely to be surpassed. In collaboration with designers, developers and dynamicists such as Arthur Carroll, Bill Lacey and Leo Kusmicki, he sent forth from the Bracebridge Street race shop a line of machines that all had the stamp of his

—and every true engineer's—philosophy: 'if it is going to work well it must be simple'. It was said of Joe Craig that he possessed 'a blotting-paper-like ability to absorb information, and adapt it to his own ends, which provided the most potent weapon in the Craig armament'.

He was buried near The Hague in Holland. His wife—as a widower he had not long been re-married—escaped from the car accident and is the donor of the TT's Joe Craig Trophy, given for the best aggregate performance by a British rider.

As the racing season approached, Bracebridge Street let it be known that there would be no factory entries for 1957, but 'unofficial' works machines would be available and there would be no objection to their being streamlined if the entrants wished.

Using 'unofficial works' machines in both the Junior and Senior TTs the riders and entrants nominated were Jack Brett (Lord Montagu), Alan Trow (Reg Dearden) and John Hartle (Eric Bowers, a dealer in John's home town, Chapel-en-le-Frith).

Costing £480 each, the production Manx models had re-designed con-rods, big-end and crankpin assemblies, coarser pitch bevel gears, sodium-cooled inlet valves, bigger bore carburettors and, for 350s, the new inlet cam.

This was the Golden Jubilee TT meeting and the Norton singles were up against highly potent German and Italian machinery, including the fearsome Guzzi V8. In the Junior the Norton team came adrift. Hartle fell on a patch of oil on the fourth lap while dicing with Dickie Dale for the lead. Brett went out with engine trouble on the last lap and Trow finished tenth.

In the Senior there was a real surprise for, when the trio—with Jackie Wood deputising for Hartle, still injured from his Junior spill—weighed in they declared engine dimensions of 90 mm × 78.48 mm, 498 cc. In other words the experimental department's Doug Hele had resurrected Joe Craig's 1954 '90 bore' outside flywheel layout, but had returned the flywheel inside the crankcase. All three machines were fully streamlined, though with different types according to the entrants' own arrangements.

There had been possibilities of a new Norton system of desmodromic valve gear but this was not used.

The motorcycling world knows that the Golden Jubilee Senior TT saw the attainment of the long-awaited 'ton'. Bob McIntyre, the winner, actually put in four laps on his Gilera at over 100 mph, his fastest being at 101.12 mph.

That the '90 bores' had speed was demonstrated by Jack Brett who, when he fell on the seventh of the eight laps, had already turned a circuit at 97.5 mph. Trow was sixth—the first all-British combination of man and machine. Among the 13 off-the-leader board riders that obtained replicas, all but two were Manx-mounted.

To round off the Jubilee week Eric Oliver, with Stan Dibben as passenger, drove his 1954 Norton-Watsonian sidecar outfit round the Mountain Circuit on a closed roads 'lap of honour', averaging 73.62 mph!

In the Belgian GP Brett, Australia's Keith Bryen and Kentish short-circuiter Derek Minter pulled off a Norton 1-2-3 after the 'winner', Libero Liberati (Gilera), had been disqualified.

Manxman Alan Holmes took Dearden-prepared Nortons to a double Manx GP victory.

For 1957 the standard range was extended by the introduction of a new twin-cylinder machine, the Model 77, which was a version of the 597 cc type specially intended for sidecar work and having a brazed-up frame without the long-used engine cradle casting. This frame was also used for the three single-cylinder machines, all of which had newly designed heads incorporating separate cast-in valve chambers and improved fin disposition. The models 88 and 99 also had re-designed heads with better finning between the exhaust ports. More efficient, full width hub-type brakes were generally adopted.

1958

This was the firm's Diamond Jubilee—60 years since the founder registered his Norton Manufacturing Co in 1898. To celebrate the occasion the first quarter-litre Norton was introduced, the Jubilee 250, with separate parallel, forward-sloping cylinders of 60 mm × 44 mm (249 cc) topped by a one-piece ohv head. The four-speed gearbox was in unit with the crankcase and an AC generator was inbuilt on the nearside. This power unit owed its inspiration to Bert Hopwood, but 'head office' pressures from Plumstead required the use of certain components such as frame parts, brakes and enclosing panels from other sources in the AMC group. The Jubilee model did not actually make its appearance until the 1958 Show, when it joined a stock range for the coming season that was changed only in that the models 88 and 99 had AC generators.

It was in February of this year that Gilbert Smith resigned. When he joined Nortons in 1916 he was one of a staff of four, and 42 years later he handed over his managing directorships of Norton Motors Ltd and R. T. Shelley Ltd to Bert Hopwood.

Racing policy, it was announced, would not include the entry of works teams but 'as new projects are developed they will be tested in competitive events'. Manufacture and development of Manx racers would continue with service facilities available at Bracebridge Street and at the TT.

Among the 'new projects' introduced in time for the TT were a revised version of the gearbox and an even bigger bore for the 30M—93 mm × 73.5 mm. There was also an experimental 80 mm bore Junior model with a five-speed gearbox. Furthermore, one of the 500 cc motors was built with an outside flywheel.

For the Island the new engines were shared out among Reg Dearden entries Keith Campbell, Alan Holmes, and (350 only) Geoff Duke. R. N. 'Bob' Brown, entered by the ACC of Australia, also had one of the 93 bore motors.

As it happened, neither the 80 bore 350 nor the outside flywheel 500, which was allotted to sidecar man Pip Harris, was used in the races. The Junior event was a run-away victory for John Surtees (MV) but the tussle for the other leaderboard places was an all-Norton affair between Dave Chadwick, Geoff Tanner, Terry Shepherd, George Catlin and Alastair King, ending in that order. And the Senior pattern was very much the same, the places after Surtees being filled by a Norton quintet consisting of Bob Anderson, Bob Brown, Derek Minter, Dave Chadwick and J. D. Anderson.

In neither race was the Manufacturers' prize awarded.

1959

Towards the end of the 1958 season Alan Holmes race-tested an engine that was obviously different externally from previous Manx types, in that the vertical drive to the cam gear was enclosed in a tube that extended straight down to the lower bevel box, eliminating the long-familiar turret bearing housing. More precise details of this change were revealed early in the new year. Instead of the old method of running the drive shaft in bronze bushes and using Oldham couplings to correct misalignment, the shaft was now supported at both ends in splined members and carried on needle roller bearings. Alterations to the cam box to accommodate this new system were made and a plain inlet valve replaced the sodium-cooled component. A revised clutch with the friction material on the driven plates was adopted, as well as a new pattern Lucas racing magneto. In the layout of the new engine the possibility of incorporating desmodromic valve gear was borne in mind.

In the spring Edgar Franks, who in pre-war years had much to do with the design detail of both road- and race-going Nortons, left to join Kaye Don in the production of Ambassador motorcycles. His technical duties at Bracebridge Street were taken over by Alan Wilson.

The TT saw the first, and only, Formula 1 event, a three-lap Mountain Circuit race jointly for 500 and 350 cc standard racing motorcycles. The larger class was almost entirely an all-Norton

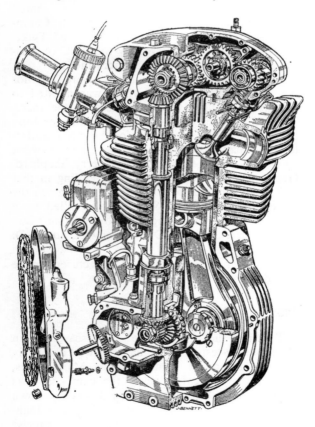

The Manx engine as it was being built in 1957—with coarse pitch bevels and a redesigned crank assembly having a sleeved big-end eye. Both valves were sodium cooled and the piston was flat topped.

event, only two out of the 15 finishers, the seventh and the last men, being mounted on other makes of machine. Bob McIntyre was the winner at 97.77 mph. The 350 honours were shared fairly equally between Norton and AJS riders, Alastair King (AJS) beating Bob Anderson (Norton) by a 20-second margin.

Although a 'desmo' 500 was given a pre-race airing by Terry Shepherd it was not used for racing; nor was the experimental short-stroke 350. In both the Junior and Senior races the MVs of John Surtees were uncatchable, but Alastair King had a good week with his Joe Potts's Nortons coming third to Hartle in the Junior and second to Surtees in the Senior, which had been postponed because of bad weather and was still held under such atrocious conditions that the winning speed was the slowest for a 7-lap Senior since 1949.

For non-racing people, the Norton range for 1959 adopted AC generators throughout and the ohv singles lost their brazed-up frames, being Featherbed types. The Model 19S was dropped from the programme.

1960

The year was but a month old when the company announced further improvements to the Manx models—modifications that applied equally to the 350 and 500 cc types.

Externally the innovations were few. A glass fibre frontal cowl provided a number plate area and supported a Perspex screen as well as shrouding a 9,000-rpm indicator. Glass fibre was also used to form the base of a new seat which weighed only 2 lb 7 oz as against the 6¼ lb of the former metal-based type. The part of the exhaust megaphone that was previously flattened to aid cornering was now fluted to resist vibration. A close look at the rear hub would have revealed the use of longer and larger diameter dowels to provide a more rigid six-point engagement with the sprocket. A new method of securing the oil tank with a strap was used.

Chief of the internal changes concerned the connecting rod, the eye of which was broadened from ¾ in to 1 in, with appropriate changes to the roller bearings and their cage. The bronze drive side thrust ring between flywheel and big end, hitherto secured in its recess by countersunk screws, was made eccentric to prevent rotation without weakening the flywheel by drilling and tapping screw holes.

The pent at the crown of the piston was raised

In a single season—1962—Manx 30M (500 cc) and 40M (350 cc) production racing machines were credited with no fewer than 760 first places. Although quantity construction ceased in 1961, special order models were built for a further two seasons, reaching the stage shown in this drawing which appeared in Norton catalogues for 1963.

by $\frac{1}{8}$ in to increase the compression ratio from 10.6 (348 cc) and 10.07 (499 cc) to 11 : 1 for both engines. With a chrome-plated top ring, the piston was lightened and non-rotating circlips locked the toughened gudgeon pin which was made of nitrided steel. Allen-type socket screws replaced the cheese-headed ones used to secure the timing side main ball bearing journal. Stellite-tipped tappets superseded the former case-hardened units.

A more positive method of attaching the clutch to the gearbox mainshaft was adopted and gear changing was made easier by shortening the pedal linkage. A revised 'damped weir' Amal GP carburettor was fitted and the wheel rims had serrations on their inner surfaces to prevent tyre creep and to dispense with security bolts.

The chief innovation in the roadster range was the provision for the de luxe models 88 and 99 of rear enclosure panelling on the lines of the 250 Jubilee. The Featherbed frames were modified along the top rails to take a new-shape tank, narrowed at its rear to allow the rider's knees to tuck in more closely.

At the TT, Norton produced a 350 cc version of the previous year's Senior desmodromic engine. It made only a brief showing during practising. Almost equally short was a try out by

Eddie Crooks of a remarkable experiment which came to be known as the Lowboy. This machine, designed specifically to obtain a very low centre of gravity, had the tank mounted between the top rails of the Featherbed frame and behind the engine. The rider's chin pad was virtually on top of the cambox. As a normal front fork assembly would have impeded forward vision, a pedal cycle-type column was used with the stanchions rising no higher than the crown lug.

On their Italian MVs Surtees and Hartle shared the Junior and Senior race honours. In the latter event ten of the first dozen places were taken by Norton riders, headed by Mike Hailwood. He and Derek Minter both made history by putting up the first two laps ever to be covered at over 100 mph on British single-cylinder machines, 100.37 and 101.05 mph respectively.

Towards the end of the year a cheaper 250 Jubilee Standard was introduced which dispensed with the enclosure panelling. An export-only 650 cc Dominator machine named the Manxman was introduced, and an eve-of-Show surprise was a 350 cc version of the Jubilee named the Navigator.

1961

'Just like old times!' the fans cried gleefully

as they came away from the TT races. They had seen a Norton Junior/Senior double and—for the first time since 1950—a Senior hat-trick for the silver tankers! There was an added bonus for home pride in the fact that the first push-rod engine machine ever to clock a lap at over the ton was also a Norton.

It has to be remembered, of course, that in this year the Italian manufacturers had signed a non-participation agreement. Even so, MV-Agusta had circumvented the treaty by providing what were called 'Privat' machines, and Gary Hocking was all set to win the Senior on one of these when it broke down after he had made the fastest lap.

In winning, Mike Hailwood, whose Norton was Lacey-tuned, created another record—for the first time a British single completed the seven-lap race at over 100 mph. Bob McIntyre, who was second on a Joe Potts-prepared model, just missed the ton, averaging 99.20 mph.

These mighty efforts were almost overshadowed by the performance of the third man home, Australian T. E. Phillis. His machine was an entirely new Norton production prototype, the Domiracer, based on the Dominator 88 and kept a closely guarded secret until the eve of the TT.

Main changes from standard practice were seen in the use of a lightened Featherbed frame which was shorter and lower, increased downward angle for the inlet ports and a Swedish-made five-speed gearset in a normal Norton box. At 283 lb, 35 lb less than the normal Manx model, the Domiracer had originally been developed for Daytona where earlier it had been given a trial by Mike Hailwood. After some four years of development work on it, Doug Hele was

reported to express the belief that 'it would give a good account of itself in serious racing'. Tom Phillis had the opportunity of covering only a few practice laps on this prototype before he started in the Senior race. He topped the ton on his second lap—100.36 mph, which was actually faster than Bob McIntyre's best circuit.

Slackening of tappets and trouble with the rear tyre touching the fork caused Phillis to keep a close rein on his speed, yet his final circuit was the only one, apart from the fill-up lap, which was completed in over 23 minutes. He averaged 98.78 mph and, had he had a more suitable tyre size, he would undoubtedly have done better, for it was found that the rev output was a thousand down on what had been achieved in experiments at MIRA.

This smashing Senior 1-2-3 followed a nearly similar Junior success in which the first English TT victory since 1952 was achieved on a privately owned Norton ridden by a TT newcomer, Phil Read. He beat Hocking's MV by 56 seconds. Ralph Rensen and Derek Minter brought Nortons into third and fourth places.

Those enthusiasts who cheered this double-barrelled Norton comeback were not to know that, so far as the TT was concerned, the famous Manx models had fired their last on-target shots. Doug Hele produced modifications for the Ulster Grand Prix which included a new type of dual shoe front brake and it was expected that the Domiracer would be available for the 1962 season. In fact, it was never sold over the counter, and manufacture of 30M and 40M types virtually ceased at the end of 1961. A few, to very special order, were assembled from existing stocks of spares, but in 1963 AMC finally stopped selling racing motorcycles.

62: *Bracebridge Street mechanic Charlie Edwards (in raincoat) introduces John Surtees to the machines he was to ride in the Junior and Senior races of 1954, the first of the two years he spent under Nortons' banner.*

63: *The backbone of the Norton ranges since Edwardian times, the side-valvers made their last appearance in 1954. Contrast the stark machine in picture 7 with this good-looking, completely equipped 16H, which bowed out still having the 79 mm × 100 mm, 490 cc, configuration.*

64: *A double-knocker 'Joe Motor' pokes its head out of a Formula 3 racing car while constructors Francis Beart and John Cooper discuss it with Stirling Moss at the Silverstone Daily Express Trophy meeting, May 1954.*

65: *A 1955 memory of Clypse Course sidecar racing. L. W. Taylor leads F. Taylor, both using Norton-Watsonian outfits, through the Nursery bends.*

66: *Using 'over-the-counter' Manx models, the Norton Slazenger team of John Hartle (second), Jack Brett (third) and Alan Trow (seventh) won the 1956 Senior Manufacturers' Award. Trow is here seen bump starting.*

67: *Although offered a Gilera for 1956, Bob McIntyre remained loyal to his tuner-sponsor Joe Potts, on whose pannier-tanked Senior Norton he is here rounding Waterworks Corner.*

68: *Mike Hailwood rounding Signpost Corner on his Senior Norton during the 1961 TT. He went on to win the Trophy at a race average of over 100 mph. No other single cylinder motorcycle has ever achieved this.*

69: *Australian Tom Phillis in 1961 was the first rider to lap the TT course at over 100 mph on a push-rod machine—the new Domiracer twin, here seen flat out at the foot of Bray Hill. Hailwood, McIntyre and Phillis brought Nortons' score of TT hat-tricks up to 12.*

70: *George Kerker (750 Norton) winning a Superbike Production Machine Race at Carlsbad, San Diego, California, in April 1971.*

71: *The 1972 version of the Commando racer as used by the John Player-Norton team.*

72: *Developing 65 bhp at 6,500 rpm with its new Combat engine, the latest in the line of Norton Commandos - the 1972 Interstate - combines handsome lines with roadburning performance.*

73: *Three aspects of the 1973 John Player Norton monocoque racer. Ridden by Peter Williams and Mick Grant, models were first and second in that year's Formula 750 IoM race, Williams averaging 105.47 mph with a fastest lap at 107.27 mph.*

74: *With a swept volume capacity of 600 cc, the NVT Wankel engine is air-cooled and has two relatively small rotors; using low-grade fuel, it develops 65-70 bhp at 8,000 rpm.*

75: *As an unfaired roadster, fully silenced, this Wankel-engined NVT prototype covered seven consecutive laps of the 2.8 mile MIRA circuit at an average speed of 131 mph.*

76: *A single, large-diameter frame member, incorporating the fuel tank, constitutes the backbone of the NVT prototype 50 cc moped. Designed specifically for economy transport, with 150 mpg averages, it weighs 200 lb.*

77: *With all the attributes of a sports-competition machine, this 125 cc single-cylinder two-stroke NVT innovation includes a gas-filled mono-shock rear frame, five-speed gearbox and hydraulic front disc brake.*

78 & 79: (*Above, left and right*) *Combining a five-speed, crossover gearbox, chain driven on the right side, the Cosworth engine for the new Norton Challenge model is a water-cooled, 8-valve, dohc, parallel twin of 743.4 cc, developing 115-120 bhp at 10,500 rpm.*

80: *First track appearance of the Norton Cosworth Challenge was in the International Powerbike race at Brands Hatch on October 25 1975, when, ridden by Dave Croxford, it was involved, and damaged, in a nine-machine pile-up at Paddock Bend on the first lap. This picture was taken during the practising period.*

Chapter 26

Goodbye to Bracebridge Street!

NORTONS to leave Bracebridge Street! The shock headline hit the papers in mid-July 1962, and an astonished motorcycling public reacted as if told that the apes were deserting Gibraltar's Rock. Since 1920 the complex of factories straddling three north Birmingham thoroughfares, known world-wide as 'Bracebridge Street', had symbolised a foundation on which British motorcycle supremacy was built.

The shattering announcement was made by A. A. Sugar, AMC Group managing director, who also revealed that the associated R. T. Shelley business would be moved to the James premises at Greet. Alec Skinner had resigned his dual managing directorship of both Norton and Shelley. Norton was to be amalgamated with Matchless Motorcycles Ltd, of Woolwich, within 12 months.

This 'rationalisation', as it was called, of the AMC Group's empire was, perhaps, not much of a surprise for those people who really had their ears to the ground. During the latter half of the 1950s the effects of the international General Agreement on Trade and Tariffs (GATT) were severely felt, for the protection against foreign imports, enjoyed since the Second World War, had been virtually withdrawn and Britain's motorcycle makers, from being world leaders, had been driven into a fierce commercial struggle. At the end of 1961 AMC Ltd had announced that its previous year's profit of £219,000 had turned into a loss of £350,000.

By this time the Group, which had never interested itself in either the moped or scooter markets, was facing seriously diminishing sales of its own small-engined James and Francis-Barnett models. At first, manufacture of the AMC-designed two-stroke units was discontinued, only machines with Villiers engines being offered. Then production was wholly concentrated on four-strokes, with the emphasis on bigger and bigger capacities.

The Manxman 650 cc version of the Dominator, primarily introduced for North American consumption, was made available to the home market in Standard, Sports and De Luxe forms. The Norton catalogue for 1963 was the last to be issued from Bracebridge Street.

The 650 cc types were quickly followed by an even larger machine, the Atlas, first made for export only but also listed as a police model. With bore and stroke dimensions of 73 mm × 89 mm, 745 cc, it developed nearly 50 bhp and had a flexible 10 to 100 mph performance on its 4.53:1 top gear.

The move from Birmingham to Woolwich was made during 1963 and the catalogue for 1964 carried the imprint 'Norton Motor Cycles Ltd, 44 Plumstead Road, London SE 18'. It listed a small range consisting of standard versions only of the 250 cc Jubilee and 350 cc Navigator, the 500 cc 88 and 650 cc Sports Special and a newcomer, a 400 cc edition of the Jubilee type called the Electra ES400, which was equipped with an electric starter.

The range for 1965 looked as though someone had taken a collection of AMC, Jubilee and Featherbed frames, AJS, Matchless and Norton engines and, with name plates for all three marques, shaken them up in a giant hat to produce 22 varieties of single- and twin-cylinder ohv motorcycles.

The Nortons in this miscellany were the Jubilee, the Navigator, the ES400, a Mk II and an ES Mk II (virtually 350 and 500 cc AJS/Matchless machines with Norton tank symbols), the 500 and 650 cc Sports Specials and the Atlas.

For the 1966 season the Norton content was reduced to six machines by the dropping of the Navigator and the ES400.

In August of that year, the AMC management found itself unable to carry on and a receiver was appointed by the bank. In September, terms had been agreed for the takeover of the business by Manganese Bronze Holdings, which had taken over the Villiers Engineering Company the previous year. These acquisitions were merged into the Villiers Engineering Company and the name changed to Norton Villiers, with former racing driver Dennis Poore, chairman of Manganese Bronze, as its chairman, and John Neville, vice-chairman of Manganese Bronze, in charge of motorcycle affairs at Plumstead.

In an introduction to Gregor Grant's book *AJS: The history of a great motorcycle* (published by Patrick Stephens Ltd, Cambridge, at £2.95 net),

F

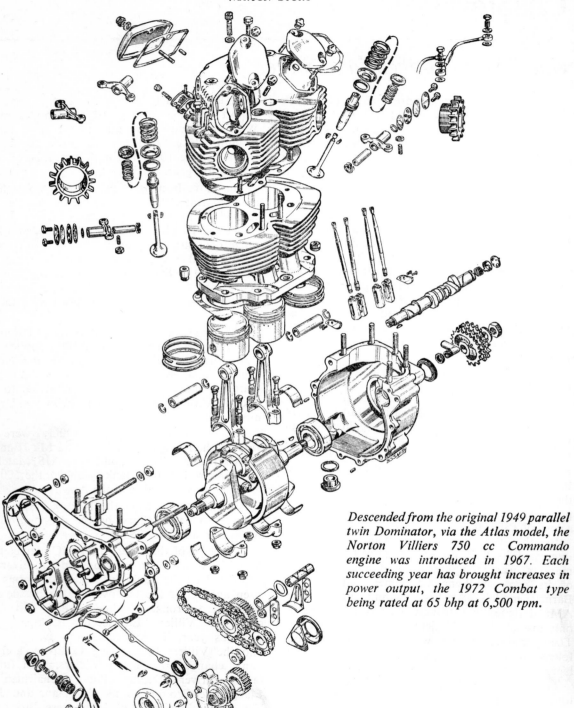

Descended from the original 1949 parallel twin Dominator, via the Atlas model, the Norton Villiers 750 cc Commando engine was introduced in 1967. Each succeeding year has brought increases in power output, the 1972 Combat type being rated at 65 bhp at 6,500 rpm.

Dennis Poore has set on record the background to these changes.

'By 1961', wrote Poore, 'Associated Motor Cycles Limited, the once proud home of so many famous marques, was languishing under a heavy burden of debt. The Villiers Engineering Company Limited, which had been the foremost supplier of small petrol engines for industrial and motorcycle use since most people could remember, was facing severe competition from American and Japanese imports; its profit and loss account was telling the inevitable tale.

'What was to be done to rejuvenate this vital industry so that it could resume its proper place on the British scene? The answer proposed by my colleagues on the Manganese Bronze Holdings group board was a marriage of these two companies within our group. The financial implications were studied, obstacles overcome and the

bold concept of this plan was started in 1962. By 1966 it had been consummated and Norton Villiers Limited was born.'

During the course of 1966 all machines (with the exception of about 100 Matchless 500 cc singles) were of 650 or 750 cc, that is the Featherbed-framed 650 SS and the Atlas 750, the Matchless-framed Norton N15 and the Matchless G15 — both the latter having the 750 cc twin engine.

Introduced for 1967 was the Norton P11A, an all-purpose mount intended for street or competition work and having the Atlas power unit in a lightweight scrambles frame. For the following year this machine, in re-styled form, became the Ranger and at the same time the 650 SS was reshaped as the Mercury.

It was on January 1 1967 that Dr Stefan Bauer joined Norton Villiers from Rolls-Royce to head a technical team briefed to produce an entirely new Norton model—to be called the Commando. Associated with Dr Bauer in this exercise were two motorcycle development engineers, Bernard Hooper and Bob Trigg, whose concept of a new form of engine mounting—the now well-known Isolastic principle—later won them the 1969

The Commando frame, which replaced the Featherbed type, employed a main top member of 2½-in diameter by 16 gauge tube and the complete assembly, immensely rigid, weighed only 24 lb. The layout of the patented Isolastic system of mounting engine and swinging fork pivot together in a rubber suspended sub-frame is clearly shown in this drawing.

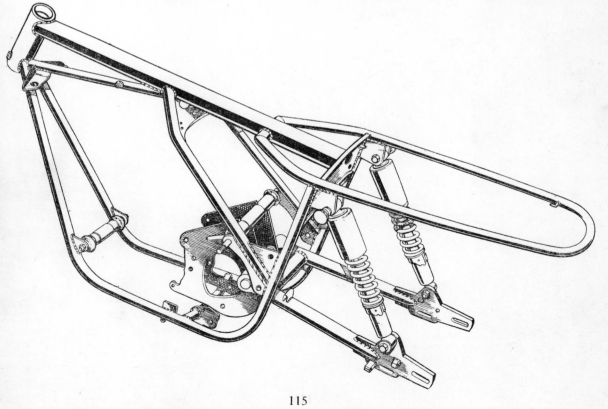

Ferodo £1,000 award for the most meritorious contribution to motorcycling.

The first Commando, given the name Fastback, had a general specification that was to continue as the basis of Norton machines henceforward. An Atlas-type engine was set in an inclined position in a sub-frame unit. Engine, gearbox (triple row roller primary chain) *and* the pivot bearing for the swinging rear fork were all carried in the sub-unit which was suspended fore and aft on three rubber bushes attaching to the main frame. This Isolastic arrangement provides a remarkably smooth cushioning effect in damping engine vibration. The main frame, though using a conventional twin tube cradle to support the sub-assembly, was unlike the Featherbed in that a single $2\frac{1}{2}$ in diameter thin gauge member acts as a 'top tube' from fork crown to the seat struts. Thus, resistance to frame twisting is achieved by virtue of the strength of the top member without the need for heavy gauge engine/transmission mountings. Roadholder-type front forks were used in conjunction with Girling rear suspension units.

Amal carburettors supplied the gas from a still-air chamber and intake silencer. Glass fibre was employed for the tank and, on Fastback models, for the rear component which embodied the seat, registration number plate and the rear lamp cluster. Various compression ratios were available, the original figure being 7.6:1. An interesting feature was the Zener-diode capacitor ignition system which provided sparks without relying on the battery.

An early public appearance of the prototype Commando was at the 1967 Production TT and the first, export-only, 'ready-for-the-road' model made its debut at that year's Earls Court Show where, in all its polished, silver-sheen glory, it gladdened the eyes of the crowds who saw in the Fastback a notable Norton comeback.

Chapter 27

Modern Times

MEANWHILE, what had been happening to the large numbers of Norton riders still battling on with their Manx models? We left them, in Chapter 25, coping by themselves without factory support and with increasing problems in obtaining spares.

Now into even greater prominence came the specialist tuners and sponsors, folk like Bill Lacey, Francis Beart, Steve Lancefield, Reg Dearden, Bill Stuart and Paul Dunstall. In his Leighton Buzzard workshop, engineer-sponsor Sid Mullarney could show you Ray Amm's kneeler frame, parts of a desmodromic cylinder head and a four-valve head of his own devising, as well as the Heenan and Froude water brake that formerly helped Lacey to prepare his machines. At Farnborough, in Hampshire, Beart's one-time manager, Ray Petty, worked wonders to keep the double-knocker in the picture—to such good effect that it was on one of his Nortons that Percy May became the 1971 British 500 cc road race champion.

But the Norton boys were hard put to keep their singles within sight of the flying foreign multis. Even so, they came close to TT wins on several occasions. In 1962 Beart's Senior model, ridden by Ellis Boyce, was second to a non-stop Gary Hocking (MV) and Fred Stevens (Norton) was third.

A Junior Manufacturers' team award was a Norton prize in 1963, won by Joe Dunphy, Jack Ahearn and Brian Setchell. The following year produced a second place for Derek Minter's Norton to Hailwood (MV) in the Senior.

Italy's ace, Giacomo Agostini, came on the TT scene in 1965 to back up MV's No 1, Mike Hailwood. The Norton contingent in the Senior included Minter, Ahearn, Dunphy, Griff Jenkins and John Cooper, all on finely prepared 'bangers'. After 'Ago' had retired and Hailwood had spilled and damaged his machine it began to look as though Joe Dunphy had a chance of ringing up the first Norton victory since 1961. But, under terrible weather conditions, Hailwood, averaging more than 90 mph on three cylinders for the last two laps, held off the threat. Dunphy was the only other rider to hold a 90 mph average through the race. That year both the Junior Manufacturers' and the Club team awards went to Norton trios—Chris Conn, Dan Shorey and Rex Butcher in the

former category and Jenkins, Butcher and Ron Chandler in the latter.

Chris Conn took third place in both Junior and Senior races in 1966. Apart from his Nortons, the only other British machines to figure in the first three among the meeting's six races were the AJS of Peter Williams, second in the Junior, and the Villiers of Peter Inchley, third in the 250 cc Lightweight event.

It was in 1966 that the Woolwich factory sold off completely all its racing equipment. Manufacturing rights were bought by Matchless sidecar exponent Colin Seeley, who subsequently re-sold the Norton side to another racing 'chairman', John Tickle. Some three tons of original Bracebridge Street jigs were included in the deal and, in modern workshops near St Neots, Huntingdonshire, Tickle set about producing much-needed Manx spares as well as building racers to his own design.

Diamond Jubilee TT year 1967 saw 'Mike-the-Bike' Hailwood set his famous lap record at 108.77 mph. His Senior Honda Four brought him his third Trophy in one week, taking his total of TT victories to 12—two up on Stanley Woods's pre-war score of ten. British machines figured well among the finishers. After Agostini's MV blew up on the fifth lap, Peter Williams (Matchless) held second place ahead of Steve Spencer's Lancefield Norton. A tight fight between the Nortons of John Cooper and Chris Conn ended in a fourth berth for Cooper when Conn's gearbox mainshaft broke on the last lap.

The Diamond Jubilee was introduced by a new series of production machine events for 750, 500 and 250 cc classes. Paul Smart, on a Dunstall Norton Domiracer, came second to John Hartle's Triumph in the big race.

Starting to phase out all the other models, Norton Villiers entered the home market with the Commandos in May 1968, and a Dunstall-prepared machine, ridden by Ray Pickrell, put the Norton name back among Island winners when it took first place in the 750 cc Production Race. An uncustomised Atlas, in the hands of Billy Nelson, was second.

Tony Rutter was the first Norton rider home in the 1968 Junior TT, in 13th place. In the Senior the marque had two leader-board places, Barry

Randle finishing third behind Agostini and Brian Ball (Matchless), and Kelvin Carruthers taking sixth spot.

Although Commandos were showing up well in PR events elsewhere, they were out of luck in the Island in 1969. It may well be that this was because the company was busy in other directions. In the summer of that year the Woolwich plant was finally closed down as a motorcycle factory, although it was retained for a period as a spares depot.

In the autumn engine building and all machining work was transferred to the Villiers factory in Marston Road, Wolverhampton. At the same time Norton Villiers opened up new premises at Walworth, Andover, Hampshire, close to the Thruxton race circuit where a test-development department was soon established. The new factory was a 20,000 sq ft single-storey building devoted to assembly, dispatch and service, and the first machines left there early in 1970. A second, similar bay was opened alongside the first in March 1970.

Early in 1969 the position of managing director of Norton Villiers Ltd had been assumed by Philip Sellars, and in the latter part of the year William Colquhoun, son of Dennis Poore's predecessor as chairman of Manganese Bronze, took charge of the newly formed Norton Villiers Corporation in Long Beach, California, with the Norton franchise for seven western states, formerly held by the Berliner Motor Corporation.

In May 1970 Dennis Poore himself became managing director of Norton Villiers in addition to continuing as chairman. William Colquhoun and John Pedley, director of production, were appointed to the board. On the departure of Dr Bauer for BSA, Sir Alec Issigonis—famous creator of the Mini — became the company's technical consultant.

Meanwhile, the original Fastback Commando had gained two brothers. Introduced in 1969 was the Commando S, a sports type distinguished by its high-level, cross-over exhaust pipe system, and in 1970 came the Roadster, styled for American appeal. To the great satisfaction of traditionalists, the 'curly N' insignia returned to Norton tanksides.

The 1970 sporting season began well with a convincing outright win in the May 7 Thruxton 500-mile endurance Grand Prix by Peter Williams and Charlie Sanby, who shared a very fast Commando. Sanby also took a fine first place at Anderstorp.

The effect of Williams's combination of tuning and riding skills came into full view in the Island when he and Malcolm Uphill (Triumph Trident) engaged in a titanic battle for the 750 cc Production Race title. Williams began the last lap nearly half a minute behind Uphill. The public address system and the short wave radio behind the Norton pit were checking on the gap: 20 seconds at Ballacraine, 18 seconds at Ramsey, 8 seconds at the Bungalow. The signals were flashed to Williams round the circuit. Down the Mountain was known as a favourite section for Williams, and it seemed to those eagerly listening as though he might just do it. But, when the riders crossed the line it was Uphill in front by 1.6 seconds. Those watching in the pits and grandstand had missed the final drama. A quarter of a mile from the finishing line, Williams was in front, only to find that a slight miscalculation on the fuel taken on at the pit stop had caused him to run short and to be repassed by Uphill in the last few yards.

Williams was fastest lapper, missing the magic 'ton' by a whisker—99.99 mph! Ray Pickrell, on another Commando, was third and Steve Spencer's Atlas came seventh.

The dwindling ranks of Manx models was reflected in the Junior TT wherein only half-a-dozen Nortons finished in a list of 40 replica winners. The tally in the Senior was better—19 out of 39.

On the Bonneville Salt Flats in America a Norton-powered streamliner, ridden by Sam Wheeler, attained 217 mph. At the AMDRA National Motorcycle Drag Racing Championship in Atco, New Jersey, on November 1, T. C. Christenson won the Top Fuel Eliminator with a twin-engined Norton 750 drag bike, recording 157.06 mph at the end of a $\frac{1}{4}$ mile. He also won the Junior Fuel Eliminator with a single engine Norton, recording a terminal speed of 139.10 mph.

To take care of distribution in the UK and Western Europe a new company, Norton Villiers Europe Ltd, was formed in 1971, its managing director being former Cycle and Motorcycle Association director Hugh Palin. Since 1967 he had been in charge of Norton Villiers marketing. The home sales manager's position was taken by Bob Manns who, before he had become an AMC executive, had gained fame as one of Great Britain's best trials and scrambles riders. Racing development work at the Thruxton Performance Shop was in the hands of Peter Inchley and Peter Williams, the highly successful racing son of a racing man—Jack Williams, one-time Douglas and Raleigh TT rider and later tunesmith in the AJS 'Boy Racer' heydays.

The high hopes with which the Andover camp entered the 1971 season were damped when in the Thruxton 500-miler Peter Williams dropped his

Commando within ten minutes of the end of a gruelling six-hour ride when enjoying a comfortable lead of several laps. And he was out of luck in the Island, too. In the newly introduced Formula 750 race he had to settle for a third place and in the production race event electrical trouble put him out after he had held the lead, doing one lap at the record speed of 101.06 mph. In this event he was riding an example of the 750 FIM Production Class racer which had been catalogued for the 1971 season with a 10.7 in diameter hydraulic disc front brake, a special high compression engine and a specification generally geared to track work. Another newcomer to the range that year was the Hi-rider, a high bar model designed for areas where the style was in vogue. The Commando S had made way for its successor, the SS, with high-level exhaust pipes one on each side. The Fastback, the Roadster and the Interpol police machine completed the range.

As 1971 was approaching its end, *Motor Cycle News* announced that for the fourth successive time its readers had voted the Norton Commando 'the Motorcycle of the Year'. During the season, on his racers, Peter Williams had won at Anderstorp; had been first in the Hutchinson Hundred production race at record speed, taking the Mellano Trophy; and at the Crystal Palace he had a first place at record race and lap speeds.

With a global marketing organisation well set up to meet demands for a now firmly established and very popular range of powerful 750 cc twin-cylinder motorcycles, Norton Villiers entered 1972. The experience of some five years of Commando concentration revealed that 95 per cent of production went abroad.

In January 1972 the magazine *Motorcycle Mechanics* held its Racing and Sporting Motorcycle Exhibition in London, and Norton Villiers used the occasion to introduce a new Commando, the very handsome Interstate roadburner.

In a black, gold and chrome livery, similar to that already applied to the Roadster model, the Interstate was readily recognisable by its 5½-gallon tank, disc front brake and black cylinder barrel—all standard features. The engine, named the Combat, had a compression ratio of 10:1 (the highest hitherto was 8.9:1), 32 mm choke Amal concentric carburettors (instead of 30 mm) and a highlift camshaft. A 5 bhp increase upped the power output to 65 bhp at 6,500 rpm.

All engines in the new range had, among other improvements, strengthened crankcases and roller main bearings on the timing side as well as the drive side. With the Interstate, the 1972 range

numbered six main models, the others being the Fastback, the Roadster, the Hi-rider, the special order Interpol police type and the Production Racer. Variations on the theme were available; for example, the disc brake was optional on all machines except the Hi-rider and the substitution of a four-gallon tank for the standard 3½-gallon pattern resulted in the Fastback LR (long range) machine. Other options were the fitting of the Combat engine in the Roadster machine and the availability of quartz halogen lights and flashing front and rear direction indicators.

Before the end of 1971 Norton Villiers had announced that they intended to enter the coming racing season with a full-scale team to be led by Peter Williams and under the management of a rider of great experience, Frank Perris, who would be joining the company forthwith. These were glad tidings for all Norton race fans but even more exciting news was to come the following year.

On February 3 1972, in a London hotel conference room, Dennis Poore revealed that the tobacco firm John Player and Sons had decided to sponsor the Norton race team in the Formula 750 class.

The new F750 was a mount carrying special fairing, air ducting, pannier fuel tanks and having disc front, drum rear braking. It had Lucas transistorised ignition and the engine was said to have a 7,000 rpm ceiling. In the hands of Peter Williams and Tony Rutter, it was afflicted with teething troubles in the Isle of Man but, on a Commando, Williams again secured a second placing in the 750 cc Production Race.

For the fifth successive time *Motor Cycle News* readers elected the Commando as 'the Motorcycle of the Year'.

The John Player Nortons were redesigned for 1973, the 746 cc parallel-twin engines being carried, on the Isolastic principle, in monocoque chassis built of stainless steel. Five-speed Quaife gearboxes were used and the magnesium-alloy 'artillery' wheels had double front (10 in diameter) disc brakes and a single (8 in diameter) unit at the rear. On some of the machines petrol and oil were contained in compartments constructed as part of the frame, fuel being pumped either electrically, or by mechanical means from the swinging rear fork, to a header tank.

In the Island two of these JP Nortons performed magnificently and, after his many frustrations and near-misses, Peter Williams gained a just reward when he sailed through the Formula 750 race to win at 105.47 mph with a fastest lap at 107.27 mph. And his stable companion, Mick Grant, was second, averaging 102.55 mph. In the Production Race the Commandos of Williams and Dave Croxford failed to finish, though Williams set the fastest lap speed at 100.52 mph before he went out at half-distance when in the lead. Croxford came to grief when his visor misted up and blanked off the road. He was, however, aboard the Norton that won the Thruxton 500-miler.

There were no works-entered BSAs or Triumphs in the 1973 TT, for by then the Small Heath and Meriden factories were deep in the financial troubles that resulted in the absorption, in July of that year, of the group by Norton Villiers, a government-backed operation that led to the establishment of the Norton Villiers Triumph organisation. The subsequent 18 months' 'sit-in' at Meriden and the formation of the Triumph Workers' Co-operative received so much publicity that further reference to it now would be superfluous.

NVT's plan was to concentrate production of Norton and Triumph machines at its Wolverhampton and Birmingham factories, while concurrently developing a wider range of types, aimed particularly at the smaller capacity economy field that had been left wide open to foreign manufacturers. There were, however, a number of other projects, one of which was a stepped-piston, twin two-stroke of 500 cc, named the Wulf. Designed and engineered by Bernard Hooper and David Flavill, the prototype gave a good account of itself, but was shelved while more attention was paid to bringing into being a machine which, although initially intended for racing, was envisaged as ultimately becoming a fast roadster to compete with the powerful multi-cylinder Japanese and European types. It was named the Norton Challenge, and a description of it follows later.

By 1974, however, NVT was finding the going tough; money, of course, was the chief problem, and throughout the year the general public was bombarded by the media with stories of government grants and loans, promises made and withdrawn, Ministerial and Departmental involvement and trade union intervention. With this political and financial hurly-burly ringing round them, NVT's production and racing departments pursued their paths. Embodying various improvements, Mark 2 and 2A versions of the Commando models came on the market and John Player and Commando types were prepared in the Thruxton Performance Shop. Peter Williams's 850 cc Commando survived only one lap of the 1974 Production TT but on another Commando Geoff Barry finished fourth. In the newly introduced Open Formula race, which had taken the place of the

International Senior TT as the top Isle of Man attraction, the JP Nortons of Williams and Croxford were out of the running within the first two laps, and a further blow to racing hopes came when Peter Williams later suffered such severe injuries in a crash that he was compelled to halt his brilliant, hard-fought track career.

The 1975 Norton range offered three models, the Interpol, specially equipped for police work, and the Mark 3 Interstate and 850 cc Commando types. Innovations included a solenoid-operated 12-volt starter system, a 10.7 in rear disc brake, left-side gear control, a new instrument panel arrangement and a sprung-load head steady for the adjustable Isolastic engine-mounting system. Engine details were: two cylinders, 77 mm × 89 mm, 828 cc, producing 58 bhp at 5,900 rpm with a compression ratio of 8.5 : 1. Later in the season a short-stroke 750 cc model, to be called the Norton Club, was on the stocks, specially intended for short-circuit, clubman's-type racing.

On July 17 1975 these motorcycles (except the Club model) were part of a display of NVT products and projects staged at a Royal Automobile Club press preview called by Dennis Poore 'to show the other side of the coin—things we have in fact managed to achieve despite all the trials and tribulations'. The projects on view were examples of the NVT Wankel engine, a 50 cc moped and a 125 cc lightweight motorcycle, and the Challenge engine-gear unit.

The Wankel engine was no surprise to the journalists present for it had, in the course of some five years' development, been well reported in the technical press and trial runs had been made and favourably described by a number of British and foreign rider-writers. In NVT form, the engine differs from other motorcycle applications of the Wankel 'rotary-piston' principle in that it is air-cooled and uses two relatively small rotors instead of one large component. It has a swept volume capacity of 600 cc, weighs (without gearbox) 105 lb and, on a compression ratio of 8 : 1, 65-70 bhp at 8,000 rpm is claimed, using two-star petrol. A development machine using this engine, in street form, fully silenced and without fairing, sustained seven consecutive laps of the MIRA 2.8-mile circuit at an average of over 131 mph.

The two prototype lightweight models on view were two-stroke powered and were conceived and produced in the Norton Triumph International research centre at Kitts Green, Birmingham. The moped came from the drawing board of Bob Trigg and was executed by B. J. 'Bertie' Goodman who, after the closure of the Velocette factory, became

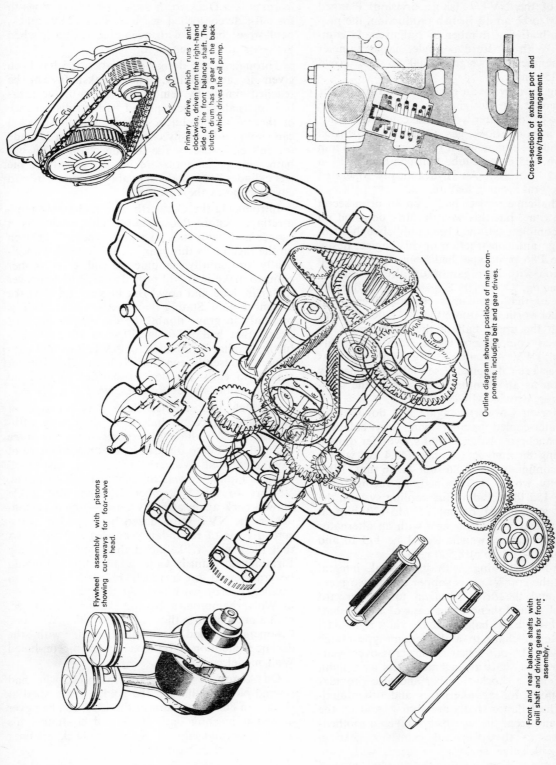

Primary drive, which runs anti-clockwise, driven from the right-hand side of the front balance shaft. The clutch drum has a gear at the back which drives the oil pump.

Cross-section of exhaust port and valve/tappet arrangement.

Outline diagram showing positions of main components, including belt and gear drives.

Flywheel assembly with pistons showing cut-aways for four-valve head.

Front and rear balance shafts with quill shaft and driving gears for front assembly.

Particularly notable among the many unusual features of the twin-cylinder Cosworth engine, designed to power the Norton Challenge model, are the Lanchester balance shafts, quill-shaft transmission shock-absorber to the inverted-tooth primary chain and belt drive for the double overhead camshafts operating eight valves.

director of the NVT Offshore division. Planned ultimately to be an all-British production, the prototype embodied a number of Italian-made components. With a sturdy, single, large-diameter frame member, it weighed 200 lb and could average 150 mpg.

Relying initially on an engine from Taiwan, the 125 cc model was designed as a sports machine adaptable to commuter work. The cantilever frame included a mono-shock, gas filled, rear suspension system and the engine was a single cylinder, 56 mm × 50 mm, 123 cc posi-lube unit combined with a five-speed gearbox. An hydraulically operated front disc brake was a feature.

The Challenge project had been an open secret for some time, but this was the first occasion on which a complete unit had been publicly exhibited. The design and construction of this engine, designated the P86 prototype, had been carried out in conjunction with an organisation already famous in car racing, Cosworth Engineering, under the guidance of that company's celebrated engineer, Keith Duckworth. To quote the NVT description: 'Although the upper half of the engine relies on well-proven components taken from the highly successful DFV Automobile Formula One units . . . it has been designed essentially for quantity production as an eventual successor to the company's present twin-cylinder range.'

The Norton Cosworth engine is a dohc, eight-valve, water-cooled parallel twin, fully balanced by two Lanchester balance shafts, cylinder dimensions being 86 mm × 64 mm, 743.4 cc; with a 'square' configuration of 86 mm × 86 mm, 1,000 cc capacity would be obtained. In racing form, weighing 155 lb including the cooling system, the P86 has a designed output of 115-120 bhp at 10,500 rpm; as a roadster unit with an alternator and electric starter, weight would be 175 lb and the output 75-80 bhp at 8,500 rpm.

A one-piece casting, with its central, integral flywheel, the crankshaft is supported on two plain journals and the drive is taken to the forward balance shaft and thence, by means of a quill shaft passing through the balance shaft, via a right-side, inverted-tooth chain to a diaphragm-type clutch and five-speed, unit-construction, crossover gearbox. The quill shaft arrangement acts as a light, low-cost engine shock-absorber and also provides a drive point for an alternator and other auxiliaries. The balance shafts are spur-geared on the left side and from the rear one is taken a toothed-belt drive to the overhead camshaft gearing. Double coil valve springs are used, with cup-shaped tappets. Among a number of other unusual features is a Duckworth design of driving dogs in the left-side controlled gearbox. This allows quick, baulk-free changes with negligible backlash when the gears are fully engaged.

Throughout the design great attention has been given to accessibility. The crankshaft can be reached simply by removing the sump; the gearbox internals can be replaced without disturbance of the engine or clutch, and the output sprocket can similarly be easily changed. Provision is made for full enclosure of the driving chain in an oil-bath. No special tools are needed to extract the wet cylinder liners and removal of plain, unstressed covers exposes the valve gear.

Introducing the Cosworth unit at the July press meeting, Dennis Poore said: 'This engine is a runner and, with luck, the prototype will be seen on the racetracks this year . . . it is intended specifically for quantity manufacture and, given proper plant to make it, it will provide the British answer to Japan, here and now.' But he went on to strike a sombre note. Stating that 'the future of NVT is presently in grave doubt', he outlined a chain of events that had led to a situation where 'unless further capital is provided for NVT, it cannot continue as presently constituted. If the Government makes no early decision or decides to take no further action, the outlook for NVT is grim.'

Through the summer there was no sign of Government succour. Indeed, a peremptory withdrawal of £4 million of export credit guarantee plunged NVT into dire straits and manufacture of Commandos at Wolverhampton was suspended when a liquidator was appointed in the autumn. Visitors to the September London Motorcycle Show—back again at Earls Court—found personnel on the NVT stand dazed by a sudden, widespread issue of redundancy notices and the news that there was a likelihood that work at the big Birmingham plant in Golden Hillock Road would be transferred on a much reduced scale to a smaller, nearby workshop. At the Villiers factory in Wolverhampton, a Norton Action Committee, with aims similar to those of the Meriden Workers' Co-operative, had established itself with the declared intention of resurrecting the pigeon-holed Wulf model.

On August 6, Walter 'Bill' Mansell, who had steered Nortons through the golden years, died at the age of 86. A spectator at the 1907 TT, he never missed a meeting until 1950, and continued his active chairmanship of the King Dick spanner company to the end of his life.

The Cosworth racer made its track debut at the

end-of-season Brands Hatch meeting. It was a brave gesture, but Fate had yet another backhander in store. The Challenge was embroiled in a first-lap, nine-machine pile-up and suffered such damage to the cooling system that it was sidelined even before it had a chance to show its paces.

On a BBC 'phone-in' programme in October, Dennis Poore advised shareholders in the British motorcycle industry not to sell out. It would survive somehow, he said, and his questioner should wait for the revival. As if on cue, came a November announcement that the Government had agreed in principle to a rescue plan for part of the NVT organisation—subject to conditions that had been put to the group and its financial advisers.

So, as 1975 drew to a close, it was on that sanguine note that the Norton Story rested. In 75 years of unbroken production, Nortons rose to 'unapproachable' heights, but they also weathered the industrial storms that have buffeted the motorcycle industry since its beginnings. When 'Pa' Norton's little business went on the rocks in 1913, it was R. T. Shelley who came to the rescue. Now, as ever-hopeful mankind embarks on the last quarter of the twentieth century, Norton wellwishers may find fresh faith in that 'trumpet's prophecy' from an earlier, more celebrated Shelley . . . 'If Winter comes, can Spring be far behind.'

Appendix

Norton successes in the Isle of Man

Class Key

T	Twin class
S	Senior
J	Junior
SC	Sidecar
F5	Formula I (500 cc)
PR	Production Race (750 cc)
F750	Formula 750 Race

TT wins by Norton motorcycles

Year	Class	Driver	Av speed mph
1907	T	H. R. Fowler	36.22
1924	S	A. Bennett	61.64
	SC	G. H. Tucker	51.31
1926	S	S. Woods	67.54
1927	S	A. Bennett	68.41
1931	S	P. Hunt	77.90
	J	P. Hunt	73.94
1932	S	S. Woods	79.38
	J	S. Woods	77.16
1933	S	S. Woods	81.04
	J	S. Woods	78.08
1934	S	A. J. Guthrie	78.01
	J	A. J. Guthrie	79.16
1935	J	A. J. Guthrie	79.14
1936	S	A. J. Guthrie	85.80
	J	F. L. Frith	80.14
1937	S	F. L. Frith	88.21
	J	A. J. Guthrie	84.43
1938	S	H. L. Daniell	89.11
1947	S	H L. Daniell	82.81
1948	S	A. J. Bell	84.97
1949	S	H. L. Daniell	86.93
1950	S	G. E. Duke	92.27
	J	A. J. Bell	86.33
1951	S	G. E. Duke	93.83
	J	G. E. Duke	89.90
1952	S	H. R. Armstrong	92.97
	J	G. E. Duke	90.29
1953	S	W. R. Amm	93.85
	J	W. R. Amm	90.52
1954	S	W. R. Amm	88.12
	SC	E. Oliver	68.87
1959	F5	R. McIntyre	97.77
1961	S	S. M. B. Hailwood	100.60
	J	P. W. Read	95.10
1968	PR	R. Pickrell	98.13
1973	F750	P. J. Williams	105.47

Clubman's TT wins by Norton motorcycles

Year	Class	Driver	Av speed mph
1947	S	E. E. Briggs	78.67
	J	D. Parkinson	70.74
1949	S	G. E. Duke	82.97
1950	S	P. H. Carter	75.60
1951	S	I. K. Arber	79.70
1953	S	R. D. Keeler	84.14

Amateur TT (1923-1929) and Manx GP wins by Norton motorcycles

Year	Class	Driver	Av speed mph
1925	500	H. G. Dobbs	59.97
1927	500	P. Hunt	57.66
1928	S	P. Hunt	67.94
1929	S	E. N. Lea	64.02
1931	S	J. M. Muir	71.79
1932	S	N. Gledhill	67.32
1933	S	H. L. Daniell	76.98
1934	S	D. J. Pirie	79.19
	J	J. H. White	75.59
1935	S	J. K. Swanston	79.62
	J	F. L. Frith	76.02
1936	S	A. Munks	78.88
1937	S	M. Cann	81.65
	J	M. Cann	76.23
1938	S	K. Bills	84.81
	J	K. Bills	78.76
1946	J	K. Bills	74.18
1947	S	E. E. Briggs	78.34
	J	E. E. Briggs	74.64
1948	J	D. Parkinson	78.20
1949	S	G. E. Duke	86.06
	J	W. McCandless	81.82
1950	S	P. Romaine	84.12
1951	S	D. E. Bennett	87.05
1953	S	D. Parkinson	89.68
	J	F. M. Fox	84.73
1954	S	G. R. Costain	80.95
1955	S	G. B. Tanner	91.38
	J	G. B. Tanner	88.46
1956	S	J. Buchan	90.83
	J	J. Buchan	88.54
1957	S	W. A. Holmes	91.43
	J	W. A. Holmes	89.13
1958	S	E. J. Washer	92.94
1959	S	E. B. Crooks	94.87
	J	P. C. Middleton	88.73
1960	S	P. W. Read	95.38
	J	E. F. H. Boyce	90.04
1961	S	E. Minihan	93.69
1962	S	P. J. Dunphy	91.38
1963	S	G. A. Jenkins	96.10
1965	S	M. Uphill	89.69
1966	J	G. B. Buchan	92.86
1967	S	J. Guthrie	94.98
	J	J. J. Wetherall	83.22
1968	S	J. T. Findlay	90.14
	J	J. T. Findlay	89.85

Index

Edinburgh, The Duke of, *84*
Edmund-JAP, *20*
Edwards, Charlie, *105*
Emde, Floyd, *74*
Emerson, Jack, *13, 35*
Evans, Don, *74, 75*
Evans, Percy, *14*

Farrant, Derek, *97*
500 Club, *76*
Flavill, David, *120*
Flook, Harold, *79, 83,*
Foster, Bob, *66, 71*
Fowler, Rem, *11, 13, 17, 18, 29, 31, 33*
Francis-Barnett, *95*
Franks, Edgar, *67, 102*
Frend, Ted, *70*
Frith, Freddie, *47, 58, 60, 61, 62, 63, 66, 69*
Frith, Julia, *47*

Gall, Karl, *61, 62*
Galway, Johnny, *61*
Garrard, Charles, *11*
Ghersi, Pietro, *39*
Gilera, *66, 71, 87, 91, 92, 95, 96, 97, 99, 100, 101*
Gledhill, Norman, *56*
Godber-Ford, Geoff, *80*
Goodman, B. J., *120*
Goodman, G. B., *38, 40, 79*
Goodman, J., *26*
Goodman, Peter, *70*
Graham, Les, *71, 93, 95*; death, *96*
Grant, Gregor, book on AJS, *113*
Grant, Mick, *110, 119*
Grinton, George, *22, 29, 31*
Guthrie, Jimmy, *37, 39, 40, 42-47, 53-61, 66, 91*; death, *61*
Guzzi, *47, 57, 58, 60, 70, 71, 75, 99, 100*

Hailwood, Mike, *91, 103, 104, 107, 117*
Half-Litre Club, *76*
Handley, Walter, *32, 45, 53, 54, 56*
Hankins, Ron, *80*
Harley-Davidson, *73, 75*
Harris, P. V., *100, 101*
Hartle, John, *98, 99, 100, 102, 103, 106, 117*
Hartwell, G. R., *76*
Hassall, Hubert, *25, 26, 27, 28, 29, 30, 34, 35, 66*

Hele, Doug, *100, 104*
Hicks, Freddie, *53*
Hill, Bobby, *75*
Hinton, Harry, *93*
Hobbs, H. E., *39*
Hocking, Gary, *104, 117*
Holden, Col H. C. L., *89*
Holliday, Bob, *46*
Holmes, Alan, *101*
Honda, *117*
Hooper, Bernard, *115, 120*
Hooton, Norman, *79*
Hopwood, Herbert, *71, 99, 101*
Horsman, Vic, *26, 27, 91*
HRD, *31, 37*
Humphries, Arthur, *80*
Hunt, Tim, *38, 39, 40, 42, 43, 53, 54, 55, 56, 68, 94*
Husqvarna, *56*

Inchley, Peter, *117*
Indian, *53, 73, 75*
International Six Days Trial, *34, 78, 83, 94*
Isle of Man TT, *see* TT Races
Issigonis, Sir Alec, *118*

James, *41, 95*
Jenkins, Griff, *117*
Judd, Rex, *26, 27, 91*

Kavanagh, K. T., *94, 95, 96*
Keeler, R. D., *96, 97*
Kerker, George, *108*
Kettle, Phil, *76*
King, Alastair, *99, 101*
Klamfoth, Dick, *74, 75*
Kretz, Ed, *75*
Kusmicki, Leo, *100*

Lacey, Bill, *32, 91, 100, 117*
Laing, Gordon, *97*
Lamb, Douglas, *40*
Lancefield, Steve, *59, 71, 73, 76, 117*
Lawton, Syd, *96*
Le Vack, Herbert, *20, 90*
Leston, Les, *77*
Letchworth, Dr G. H. S., *35, 41*
Levis, *68*
Lewis-Evans, Stuart, *77*
Liberati, Libero, *101*
Lidstone, Jack, *41*
Light Car Club, *76*

Loader, H. B., *29, 30*
Locke-King, H. E., *89*
Lockett, Johnny, *69, 71, 85, 86, 91, 92, 93*
Lomas, W. A., *99*
Long, Alf, *69*
Longman, Frank, *31, 32*
Longman H. B., *29, 30*
Lord, W. J., *29*
Lowe, R. O., *28, 68*
Luse, Tex, *75*
Lyons, Ernie, *69, 70*

Macaya, I., *23, 31, 32*
McCandless, Cromie, *24, 92, 94, 95*
McCandless, Rex, *92*
McEvoy Motorcycles, *37*
McEwan, Tommy, *69, 93*
McGill, Bill, *73*
McIntyre, Bob, *69, 91, 99, 100, 102, 104, 106, 107*
Manganese Bronze Holdings acquire AMC, *113*
Manns, Bob, *118*
Mansell, Bill, *14, 22, 23, 29, 31, 32, 37, 43, 55, 59, 62, 63*; leaves Norton, *70*; death, *122*
Mansell, D. K., *38, 40, 43, 70, 79, 83*
Mansfeld, Kurt, *61*
Manx Grand Prix, history, *68, 69*; Norton successes, *appendix*
Manx Motor Cycle Club, *28*
Masetti, Umberto, *95*
Matchless, *37, 66, 91, 95, 117*; amalgamation with Norton, *113*
Mathews, Bill, *73, 74, 75*
Matthews, H., *39*
Maudes Trophy, *28, 30, 32, 33-35*
May, Percy, *117*
Meier, Georg, *62, 63*
Mellors, Ted, *39, 59, 61, 62*
Mewis, Bill, *43, 45, 61, 70*
Milani, A., *87*
Miller, Tony, *74*
Milner, Roger, *80*
Milner, W. A. J., *80*
Minett, Denis, *82*
Minter, Derek, *101, 103, 104, 117*
Mitchell, J. L., *26*
Montlhéry, *46, 91, 95, 96*
Moore, Wally, *23, 29, 32, 40, 49, 69*; ohc engine, *36*
Morrison, George, *70*
Moss, Stirling, *77, 105*
The Motor Cycle, *34*
Motor Cycle News, *119*
Motor Cycling, *31, 66, 68, 69*

Shaw, Jimmy, *24, 26, 27, 28, 29, 36, 39, 40, 66*
Sheard, Tommy, *28*
Sheldon, Jim, *31*
Shelley, E. R., *70*
Shelley, R. T., *13, 37, 70, 123*
Shepherd, Terry, *101, 102*
Shilling, Beatrice, *90*
Shorey, Dan, *117*
Simister, Tommy, *27, 28, 29, 31*
Simpson, Jimmy, *32, 37, 40, 43, 53, 54, 55, 56*
Skinner, Alec, *99, 113*
Smart, Paul, *117*
Smith, Gilbert, *43, 66, 67, 75, 95, 98, 107*
Smith, H. G. Tyrell, *53, 54*
Smith, J., *20*
Smith, J. V., *80*
Smith, W. J., *99*
Spann, Tommy, *37*
Spencer, Steve, *117, 118*
Spring, Nigel, *34, 35, 42, 47, 53, 58, 91*
Staniland, Chris, *35, 91*
Stevens, A. J., & Co Ltd, *66*
Stevens, Fred, *117*
Stewart, Len, *36*
Storr, John, *94, 96*
Stuart, Bill, *117*
Stuart, J. A., *29, 30*
Sugar, A. A., *113*
Sunbeam, *28, 37, 39, 41, 55, 69, 79*
Surtees, John, *96, 98, 99, 100, 101, 102, 103, 105*
Swanston, Dr J. K., *44, 58, 86*

Tanner, Geoff, *101*
Taruffi, Piero, *91*
Taylor, A. E., *31*
Taylor, F., *97, 106*
Taylor, L. W., *97, 106*
Tenni, Omobono, *60, 70*
Thomas, Ernie, *59*
Thomas, William, *74*
Tickle, John, *117*
Totoraitis, Ted, *74*
Travers Trophy Trial, *40*
Trials, *78, 79*
Trigg, Bob, *115, 120*
Triumph, *14, 20, 69, 72, 117, 118, 120*
Trow, Alan, *100, 106*
TT races, first, *11, 33*; Norton placings, 1920-28, *39*; course described, *49-51*; Norton successes, *appendix*
Tucker, George, *23, 27, 28, 29, 31, 32, 81*
Tuman, Bill, *75*
Twemlow, Eddie, *30*
Twemlow, Kenneth, *30*
Tyrrell, R. K., *77*

Uphill, Malcolm, *118*
USA, Norton racing successes, *73-75*

Vandervell, C. A., *14, 70, 99*
Vandervell, Tony, *14, 20, 21, 26, 27, 70*

Velocette, *32, 47, 56, 57, 59, 60, 62, 63, 70, 71, 94*
Victory Trial, *78*
Vidal, J., *31*
Villiers Engineering Co Ltd, amalgamation with Norton, *115*

Walker, Graham, *20, 27, 28, 37, 41, 53, 54, 85, 100*
Wallach, Theresa, *90*
Watson, R. G. J., *97*
Watson, Tommy, *14*
Watsonian Sidecars Ltd, *97*
Weddell, Jock, *70*
Welsh Trophy Trial, *40*
West, Jock, *60, 61, 62, 63, 66*
Western Centre Trophy Trial, *40*
White, J. H., *57, 58, 59, 60, 61, 62, 63, 69*
Williams, Jack, *43, 56, 60, 61, 79, 118*
Williams, Peter, *110, 117, 118, 119, 120*
Williamson, Henry, *14*
Willis, Harold, *60*
Wilson, Alan, *102*
Wilson, E., *80*
Wood, Jackie, *100*
Woodhouse, Major Jack, *20*
Woods, Stanley, *24, 32, 36, 37, 38, 39, 40, 41, 43, 47, 53, 54, 55, 57, 58, 59, 60, 61, 62, 66, 117*
Wright, W. G., *59*

Young, Rex, *80*

128